Praise

'This book is the bible ____ ____ ng to adapt their goals to a pr____ ____er-first approach. Luis has redefin____ ____ needed to transform a project compan____ ____roduct company. I am going to recomme____ this book to every business owner and project manager.'
— **Neha Shaikh**, Producer – Digital and Live Events, Informa Connect

'You can't have your cake and eat it too – this is something often missed by leaders in their digital transformation plans. *Product First* lays down not just the "why" and "what" of the product approach, but also the uncomfortable "hows" – namely around leadership alignment, culture and organisational design.'
— **João Colaço de Freitas**, executive board member, Cofidis

'What a great journey. The book explains step by step how to transform your business and maximise product value creation in this digital era through innovation, agility and organisational transformation. And the creative storytelling format means you can have fun and relate this to your own experience.'
— **José Pedro Pinto**, General Manager, Arval

'Digital transformation is not just selling on digital channels. It goes much deeper, into an organisation's way of working, strategising and planning. Its mastery requires boldness from top to bottom. But it is possible. Luis brings us a methodology that helps us embrace digital transformation, brilliantly meshing frameworks, like Scrum, and techniques, like Google Design Sprint, with his own methodology, ADAPT, to create a holistic way for companies to embark on their digital transformation journey. The story presents it all in an easy, empathetic way, so that all of us can understand and feel motivated to adopt it.'

— **Rui Pedro Saraiva**, Chief Technical Officer, CTT

'*Product First* has managed to summarise twenty years of my own professional experience of doubt and certainty into one amazingly interesting story that will help any executive navigate an ever faster digital business world. This book will prove to be an absolute must for any C-level executive with ambitions not only to stay alive but to drive their business forward in a high-velocity digital world.'

— **Marcus Nordquist**, founder and CEO, Queenslab

'Inspiring storytelling in this book creates a fun way to understand the essential moves for getting into the product world. These topics are crucial for the future success of almost all companies.'

— **Henri Hämäläinen**, Deputy Board Member, Eficode

'Transformation isn't just applying proven methodologies – it comes along with the right mindset, clear direction, eagerness and motivation. In *Product First*, Luis brings everything together, providing a proven path for all of us that can easily be adapted to any organisation.'
   — **Andreas Wittge**, Senior Director Solutions and Engineering, ALDI Nord

'For the first time, Luis sets out in this book the practical method for transformation from projects to products. The journey is told through the story of fictional people who describe real situations, stressing the challenges that companies have when they realise it is necessary to change. With concrete examples, Luis has captured the step-by-step path to transform an organisation and the steps to do it with success.'
   — **Jorge Afonso**, Chief Data and Analytics Officer, Galp

PRODUCT
FIRST

Make the shift from project to product to future-proof your digital business

by Luis Gonçalves

Foreword by Mishari A Al-Assailan

R^ethink

First published in Great Britain in 2023
by Rethink Press (www.rethinkpress.com)

© Copyright Luis Gonçalves

Illustrations by Liliana Gomes

Contents

Foreword   1

Introduction   5

1 Discovery   **15**

Arrival   19

The problem   25

The proposal   31

2 Approach   **37**

Day One   39

Strategy   49

Awareness   55

Leads   59

Engagement   61

Sales   63

3 Agility   **71**

Comparing Agile and Waterfall   72

The Agile vs Waterfall exercise   93

4 Continuous Delivery   **101**

Day One reflection   111

5 Product   **113**

Day Two   114

The Business Model Canvas   118

6 Continuous Discovery   **127**

7 Organisational Mastery – Part One   **145**

Day Three   146

OM Component 1: OKRs   155

8 Organisational Mastery – Part Two   **169**

OM Component 2: Cost of Delay   169

Urgency profiles   176

OM Component 3: Impediments   189

9 Organisational Mastery – Part Three   **199**

OM Component 4: Communities of Practice (CoP)   200

OM Component 5: Design sprints   208

10 Data   **217**

The outcome   227

Conclusion   **231**

Acknowledgements   **235**

The Author   **237**

Foreword

Digital transformation is no longer a new idea. In many countries, the revolution of the digital age influences the ambitions of stakeholders, including governments and regulators, investors and business leaders. It is also heralding the rise of tech accessibility among end users and customers through the internet and smartphones. However, despite these ambitions, executing the digital agenda is still one of the biggest challenges that could face any company – small or big, old or new.

This is because, when it comes to usual operating models, decision makers tend to get scared of reinventing the wheel on how to delegate accountabilities and streamline agility within the organisation. They neglect the cost of opportunity loss and implement change management tactics, which cater only for the human work environment without re-engineering the value chain of output and the efficiency/flow of policies and procedures, data governance, profit/cost centres, customer centricity and behaviour.

Product First is more than a digital transformation book; it's a book that will help leaders to adapt their traditional project-centric businesses to product-led organisations. This change requires a quantum leap in perspective, practice and implementation. Above all, it requires full and committed buy-in at executive leadership level, along with the courage to truly transform.

Projects focus primarily on deadlines and targets, driven by the needs of departmental silos in justifying their existence and budget responsibility. This is the very opposite of accelerated value delivery. Product organisations, on the other hand, are value-led, outcome driven and evolutionary in style. They respond to change and develop understanding of their customers' problems. Continual discovery leads them to ask, 'Why would they buy it?' and 'What new features will persuade them to buy it again?'

For any business wishing to expand and scale internationally, having the ability to approach, attract and convert the marketplace into customers relies on it adopting a 'product-first' mentality, and utilizing the universal principles in each territory before it can become a truly global force that makes an impact.

Product First presents a fictional story that any executive in the digital age can relate to, learn from and be inspired by. The solutions and theories that the book discusses offer endless thought streams that will allow leaders to imagine and strike out with more confidence towards their 'innovation future'. Team chemistry and the ability to point out the true north for the organisation remain the baseline for any success; for the rest, we must continue to learn and grow our knowledge base – and *Product First* is a great book for doing just that.

Mishari A Al-Assailan
Vice President, Strategy and Partnerships, STC Pay

Introduction

With or without my contribution, there is a plethora of business books available aimed at large organisations hoping to transform both their operations and their fortunes. However, the majority of these will be aimed specifically at coaches, consultants, team leaders or individual contributors. There are fewer (if any) books aimed directly at executives that offer an understanding of what steps they need to take prior to implementing this transformational project-to-product journey. This is where my overarching approach in my books and practice differs.

I have already authored two books in this area: the first, *Organisational Mastery*,[1] describes a product development blueprint for digital product compa-

---

1   L Gonçalves, *Organisational Mastery: The product development blueprint for executive leaders* (Rethink Press, 2019)

nies, offering a practical root-and-branch application of the foundational guidelines; the second, *ADAPT*,[2] takes a more theoretical approach, in the form of a framework based on the five essential pillars of transformation. In this, my third book on the subject, I recognise that, for the most part, executives have been left out in the cold from the outset when their companies undergo the transformation from project-led to product-focused organisation, due to the unreasonable expectation that they should already know the fundamental requirements. In fact, they don't fully understand the steps they need to take and what will happen to their organisations once they set out on the path to transformation. It's a common misconception that simply because an executive heads up an organisation of 500 or more employees, they know everything. To get those answers, they must first be properly equipped to ask the right questions. This will then shape their strategic direction of travel toward organisational transformation. Helping you ask those right questions is my primary motivation for writing this book.

This book is based on the three-day practical and theoretical workshop that I provide through Evolution4All, designed to plug the executive knowledge gap. It follows the five pillars of my ADAPT Methodology™ framework and aims to provide a useful tool to executive leaders within the context of their own business, so that they understand:

---

2   L Gonçalves, *ADAPT: A leader's guide to staying relevant and being recognised in the digital age* (Rethink Press, 2021)

- The project-to-product transformational roadmap

- The prerequisites to deliver change

- The buy-in needed from the executive team to proceed with organisational transformation

The methodology itself arose from my years of experience helping clients to adapt their companies into truly digital product organisations in more meaningful and efficient ways than perhaps they thought possible, but in my early days that was never expressed as a cohesive methodology. It was only a matter of time before I realised that organisations lacked an overarching five-point strategic plan that they could implement to fully realise an organisational transformation (ie from projects to products) that included the cornerstones of:

- Digital content strategy

- Data

- Agility

- Digital product strategy

- Organisational transformation

Until that point, clients had been seeking ad-hoc Agile solutions because executives were unaware that transformation was wider than simply digital implementation and that they needed to encompass the bigger vision. Indeed, they were unaware they also needed to be part of that organisational transformation. The ADAPT process is not linear, it's modular. Certainly, to ensure its successful implementation all five pillars need to be engaged, but the interconnectedness of the pillars themselves is also important.

In my experience, knowing in advance the detail of what my transformational workshop will deliver is key to helping an executive understand and commit to that process of transformation in their own organisation. The workshop is designed to show how this will work in practice when implementing the key stages outlined in the five pillars of the ADAPT Methodology™. Knowledge, in this instance, is a powerful commodity, since it allows executives to lead from an informed position, placing them at the forefront of the incredible journey they are about to commit to with an organisational transformation that will help unlock the potential to realise an additional 20–30% revenue from the underused and untapped resources already within their grasp, before any future growth. For a business with a baseline revenue of $15m, that could mean another $3–5m not currently realised. This isn't an inflated hypothesis, it's an accurate reflection of what has been achieved by the clients that I've worked with and facilitated transformations in. These organisations have typically been established for several years within their niche, performing reasonably well and already utilising digital within their operations, yet were failing to maximise the opportunities of the digital era, leaving them with a significant revenue leakage within the range stated above. All as a result of not having a product strategic vision that truly delivers.

They may have employed dozens of Scrum masters and been familiar with Agile principles, but because the executives themselves were not fully invested in or informed enough about the potential that could be realised, the implementation remained half-hearted, and the organisation was underperforming.

Financial investment is not enough; alone, it won't prevent an organisation from losing revenue that it should be able to realise and reinvest into the business and its people. In this situation, even long-established, multimillion turnover organisations begin to fall behind. Their business models are no longer fit for purpose and they're bleeding money that could be spent on innovation, product development and serving their customer base. They start to panic as they see their customers gradually creeping away, toward their more digitally savvy competitors, the new entrants and disruptors to the marketplace that use their edge to fill their sales pipelines and reap maximum advantage.

The new brands on the block are kicking the older brands into touch with their more dynamic customer acquisition skills, generating and interrogating customer data that allows them to release new products to the market in direct response to customers' needs. More than that, the new brands understand the data, so they can anticipate what those needs will be before the customers are even aware of them. No matter how much financial muscle sits behind an established business, or how good its reputation, if will be forever running to stand still in the face of such competition. The old guard are simply not agile enough; their business model slows them down and they have little hope of ever catching up with the sprinters ahead of them that are fully adept at pushing out new software to increase their advantage. As they fall further and further behind, executives that believe that they *are* digital are left scratching their heads in frustration, wondering what they need to do to get back in the running.

The answer is simple and hiding in plain sight. They need to completely revamp their digital model, their business model and, more importantly, their organisational design. This is what scares them, because their organisation is designed in the traditional manner around silos and project management. No digital implementation will succeed fully when at every turn it faces barriers, bureaucracy and internal politics before a new product can be signed off. However, when executives learn about the five pillars of the ADAPT Methodology™, the penny drops and they see the problems clearly, one of which is the frequent habit of delegating digital transformation to management as a tick-box exercise. Crucially, they begin to understand how it can accelerate their revenue generation to put them back amongst the front runners that have outpaced them. Finally, through my workshops, even the biggest, most established organisations realise that they need to steer a different course and can see the roadmap to their survival.

How to present this roadmap based on the ADAPT Methodology™ in this book was initially a challenge. No two multimillion organisations are the same, in their strategic vision, their size or their culture. Many factors make up an organisation's internal fabric, but what struck me as a commonality among the variety of large clients that I have worked with is that their executive leaders were often the final decision makers yet didn't fully understand the practical ramifications of the decisions they were making. When their fortunes begin to fade, the buck will always stop with these decision makers, having signed off on whatever they felt to be the right course of action. No wonder this can leave them feeling out of the loop, confused and, frankly, vulnerable. For this book, I decided to pool my cumulative experience, based on my interactions and in-depth conversations with many a brilliant executive leader and get right to the heart of their universal challenges to create a fable that will take you step by step through their collective journeys.

I have chosen to share my workshop process using the example of a fictitious financial software solution company (Finance Software Solutions GmbH, or FSS) based in Berlin with over a hundred employees and an annual turnover of €50m. It's a long-established business that offers digital solutions for invoicing and payment software, but it hasn't futureproofed itself and is struggling to remain competitive, efficient and productive. While this example business may not be operating in your niche, it shares the typical business structure, management and leadership qualities that I have observed in all the organisations that I have helped to realise business transformations. As many of those did, FSS created a fantastic product for its customer base twenty years ago but, despite a few enhancements, it has lost market share, not because its product is in any way substandard; it is just no longer the right fit for its customers. More significantly, the business itself hasn't kept pace with the digital marketplace, as well as being stuck with a traditional organisational structure.

FSS's CEO, Herman Holl, has tried time and time again to introduce new measures, including Agile, into the mix, and has no idea what he needs to do next to turn his ship around. Helpfully, he *knows* that he doesn't know so has made it his mission to be front and centre of FSS's transformation and has also enrolled *all* of his senior executive colleagues on the ADAPT Methodology™ three-day workshop. He intuitively knows that a residual 'we've always done things this way, we don't need to change' mindset has become an established norm that is no longer serving the company.

This isn't the time for Herman to point the finger of blame at anyone, because inevitably the buck does stop with him. Unless he can be part of the change, it won't happen. From the 'workshops' presented in this book, Herman and FSS will gain:

- Identification and understanding of their particular organisational problems

- A plan of action to address them

- A call to action to implement the plan

- A roadmap to transform from a project company into a product company

Through this fictional recounting of my workshop process, the granular detail of my real clients' experiences remains anonymous, the core characters are unidentifiable and yet I hope they will be entirely relatable to you and your colleagues. The book follows the structure of my ADAPT Methodology™ three-day workshop, as follows:

- Day 1
  - Approach – 4 hours
  - Agility and technical excellency (continuous delivery) – 4 hours
- Day 2
  - Product and product discovery – 8 hours
- Day 3
  - Organisational mastery – 6 hours
  - Data – 2 hours

This book is my contribution to society. With it, I hope to influence more leaders to ADAPT their traditional project-oriented companies into product-centric companies, to create companies that deliver great products that people love and, above all, to create companies where people feel connected to a larger purpose, where office politics is less of an issue.

It's time now to walk through the doors of FSS. *Willkommen in Berlin!*

1
Discovery

About a month before my plane took off for the one-hour flight from Munich to Berlin, I received a message via my website shortly after I'd published my blog 'Project to Product: the move for every successful executive leader'. I'm a frequent blogger and like to regularly publish my thoughts on how to successfully build sustainable, future-proof digital product companies. Almost immediately after this blog went live, late on the same Sunday evening, a 'Herman Holl' reached out to me and requested an urgent call back. On the Monday I arranged with his PA to call him directly at 8am the following day, so I already had a sense that this was his top priority, and I was curious as to how I might be able to help. Herman, as I learned during our discovery call, was the

CEO of FSS GmbH, a company he'd founded fifteen years previously, having been made redundant from a finance-based corporate conglomerate where he was a regional product development director. After a short period of gardening leave, he'd used much of his severance package, along with the small amount of capital finance he'd raised, to go it alone and establish his own organisation in direct competition with his previous employer. In a sense, he was part of a new breed of digital disruptors, although at the time that wasn't recognised as the phenomenon it is today. In every sense, he was the epitome of an ambitious entrepreneur in his mid-thirties, hungry for success and with a vision to dominate the marketplace within his niche – third-party off-the-shelf financial software solutions for organisations that didn't have the infrastructure to implement this themselves.

The first ten years of operation saw FSS's reputation build and build. Its rise was meteoric, aided by the fact that in the recovery period following the global financial crisis of 2008, there were literally hundreds of new digital business start-ups establishing themselves on a daily basis – solopreneurs, partnerships, small teams of tech-savvy individuals that grasped the opportunities that the rapidly growing and fast-paced digital marketplace had to offer, opening up avenues to create new products and reach new clients that had simply never existed before. Herman and FSS were at the forefront of the new digital revolution and the future seemed bright and prosperous.

Until, as every bubble must, it burst. As Herman explained to me in his calm, measured tones over the phone, FSS had started to flatline a couple of years previously and was increasingly looking like it was about to downturn even further and head into decline. I listened attentively to the story – an all too familiar one – of how his operations director had engaged highly paid Agile consultants and Scrum masters to implement leaner processes, and introduced elements of product management into the organisation that now numbered over a hundred people. Yet, for some reason nobody could fathom, the organisation seemed to be at a standstill, 'taking one step forward, then two steps back'. It seemed that it was painful for Herman to admit this out loud. He sighed, almost imperceptibly, paused a moment and in the brief silence that followed, I picked up on his frustration. It wasn't anger, just complete mystification as to why his organisation now always seemed to be on the back foot when once it was a beacon of success that others aspired to be like. Worse still, FSS was beginning to leak clients and lose market share, despite having 'embraced Agile' as the answer to all their problems.

'So, Luis,' he said, 'I really don't know what to do, or where to start, to turn this situation around. I'm not prepared to simply let this business go to the wall – there's too much at stake. I have my people's interests to think of.'

'I guess you're like a family,' I offered.

'Yes – albeit a larger one than when I started out, but my people matter to me. We still have 90% of the same people in place from day one, and our track record of staff retention as we've grown has been incredible. I can't let them down. And I'm not about to fire hundreds of them on a Zoom call like that idiot did in America. What was he thinking? That's not leadership; that's weakness. It was cruel, a crass way of handling things.'

'I agree,' I said. 'But I think with a different approach, you can definitely avoid that.'

'I should hope so.' Herman let out a laugh, seeming relieved and like he felt a little lighter, even if only for a moment. He paused before continuing, his tone once again thoughtful and serious. 'The question is, how? We've tried everything – or that's what I thought, until I read your blog. That's why I wanted to speak with you. You seem to suggest there's a way we can transform our business and become more agile than Agile. Am I right?'

'We're on the same page,' I confirmed.

'Good. Because I hate that we've become this slow, kind of dinosaur, when what we should be about is innovation, keeping pace, exciting and inspiring our clients. After all, that's how we began. Yet, for some reason, we still have these huge dependencies on different silos within the company that slow down our process of releasing software.'

'Let me guess,' I interjected, 'no one seems to understand the big picture? Sales have decreased?'

'That's exactly it,' Herman confirmed, adding, 'and everyone seems to be shifting their efforts from project to product the whole time. Each time we want to start a new development it takes us ages. Nobody can agree on anything, and everything has to be approved by each departmental head. I don't even want to think about the constant in-fighting between departments and arguments about who's responsible for paying what, thanks to our outdated budgeting process.'

'Do you think that all this internal politicking and bureaucracy is holding the business back?' I asked.

'Yes,' Herman replied simply, 'and now we're falling behind, especially with all these new kids on the block suddenly eating into our market share.'

'I think you'll find it's not as sudden as you might think. The problem seems to me to be that you've not kept pace with the market, or what digital can truly deliver.'

'That's why we need to take a good, long look into the whole organisation. Would that be something you could do, to come in and have a chat with us for a couple of hours and then we can ask you some questions? Maybe then we'll see if there's a possible match between us.'

We agreed a date on which to meet and, one month later, I touched down in Berlin, only a fifteen-minute taxi ride away from FSS's HQ in Adlershof.

Arrival

Adlershof is home to Germany's largest science, media and technology park, founded in 1991 on the site of the former Johannisthal airfield. Today, over 1,200 high-tech and innovation-led businesses are situated here, and I could see why Herman had chosen this location for FSS's HQ. Originally, he'd signed a five-year lease for one floor in a building on the edge of the site, but as FSS grew, a new ten-year lease was negotiated for a whole building that could house his one hundred employees. On my approach, I found it impressive. Close to the busy Forum Adlershof, its four-storey glass and steel frontage glinted in the early morning winter sunshine and stood out against the bright blue sky. The automatic doors swished open as I walked toward the entrance, and I introduced myself to the friendly reception staff who issued me with my temporary pass (which was an old-fashioned laminated badge on a lanyard) and I sat myself down to wait. Not that I had to wait long, and even the reception staff were surprised to see that it was Herman himself who came through the security gates to greet me. 'Boy,' I thought to myself, 'this really does mean a lot to him.' I wasn't wrong.

Herman, dressed in smart but casual chinos and a blue linen shirt – no tie, no jacket – immediately struck me as an open, easy-going type of person. He looked to be in his mid-to-late forties. He greeted me as if we were old friends, with a firm handshake and several hearty pats on the shoulder, but all geniality aside, he was direct and eager to get down to the business I'd been invited in for. He swiftly guided me to the elevator and we rapidly ascended to the top floor. There wasn't much small talk, mainly Herman outlining the agenda and who I was about to meet. I was beginning to see that bullshit wasn't part of his vocabulary, and yet I had this suspicion that despite his forthrightness, there lingered a deep-seated frustration that he couldn't make things happen the way he wanted. At least, not right now. My first impression was that this probably wasn't down to him, but perhaps more to do with people in his executive team. Maybe I would be wrong, but my intuition always clicks in when I perceive a mismatch, no matter how small, between what I see and what I hear. I didn't want to prejudge though, because after all, today was about discovery.

Sat around the huge oval boardroom table were the key members of Herman's executive team:

- Sabine (marketing): a career graduate in her mid-thirties, she'd left university in Bonn to take a marketing internship for a consumer food product brand based in Hannover. After six months, she'd been engaged full time and within five years the business had sponsored her MBA at a graduate school for economics and, as a result, she'd enjoyed several promotions leading to her managing the marketing team. After being headhunted by a pharmaceutical manufacturer in Leverkusen, she soon realised that her career trajectory was limited and so when an MBA alumni mentioned that there was a vacancy at FSS, she applied and was appointed by Herman himself. He admired her drive and ambition as well as the fact she had experience in both B2C and B2B marketing.

- Christoph (sales): in his early thirties, originally trained to be an actor in Berlin but with a scarcity of paid work, he had supplemented his income working in telesales. It was a brutal baptism of fire, but he was quick to learn on the job. His natural rapport with potential customers earned him star status amongst his colleagues and he was able to convert more pitches into sales than almost anyone else. Before too long, he was heading up his own section as well as being placed in charge of training. But a commission-based career wasn't for him and within two years he had successfully applied to be sales manager at an online B2B travel portal. His natural ability to lead soon saw him promoted to sales director and he relished the challenge of working for a digitally driven business. Having long given up his dream of becoming an actor, he became intently career-focused and when FSS announced its expansion plans and the need to fill its sales director role with someone who could dynamically shape its vision, Christoph applied. He has been in the role for the last four years.

- Leon (operations): in his early fifties, has a solid corporate track record having begun his career in procurement for a Berlin-based company that sold software solutions to the legal profession in German-speaking territories. Having undergone management training his aptitude for strategic planning and leadership saw him climb up the career ladder at a rapid pace. In the last twenty-five years, his roles have been focused on serving digital businesses. After meeting Herman at a networking event, he was invited to join FSS as its operations director with a particular emphasis on research and development in establishing improvements and defining goals for the company.

- Jonas (product development): has just turned forty-five and is the newest appointment to the executive team, having transferred across from the automotive industry twelve months previously. He oversees a small team of four working to deliver new product development projects through effective cross-functional resource planning and project management. Since revenues at FSS had been plateauing for several quarters prior to his arrival, Herman hired him specifically for his project management skills and to head up the development and launch of new products and services.

- Friedrich, 'Freddie' (IT): has been with FSS from day one and is informally regarded as Herman's 'right-hand man'. Together they built the company from scratch into a thriving enterprise in only a few years. Prior to FSS, Freddie had worked his way up to a senior position in the petro-chemicals sector staying loyal to the company that first employed him when computers and technology were beginning to revolutionise how businesses operated. With his early interest in learning how to code bespoke software, and as an early adopter of Linux, Freddie began to create a reputation for being able to identify where IT could solve and manage internal functionalities. Uncharacteristically, Freddie resigned his position as head of IT at the petrochemical giant to accept Herman's invitation to join FSS. He often tells people that Herman wanted him in the business because he represented stability, and that his background at one of the biggest companies in Germany provided the reassurance that shareholders expected, especially in the early days of the business.

I observed that everyone, apart from Freddie, seemed relaxed, almost happy to see me. Freddie was too busy pouring and stirring his coffee to turn toward me straightaway, and when he did it was with a polite, but definitely lukewarm, 'Hi, how are you?' If his hand hadn't been cupped around his hot coffee just seconds earlier, I could have sworn he was related to a fish. Still, I reserved any judgement – after all, he might have had a bad start to the day, a blazing row with his partner, a broken-down car, who knows? His demeanour had nothing to with me, how could it? I did notice, from the corner of my eye, Herman glance toward us as my firm handshake met Freddie's pale imitation. Herman then called the meeting to order, formally introduced me and why I was there, and the floor was mine.

The problem

I briefly ran through my experience and how I came to set up my company, Evolution4All, and how, over the years, I'd come to the realisation that Agile wasn't quite the panacea it's made out to be if it wasn't truly embedded within an organisation's structure. As soon as I mentioned 'Agile', Freddie let out a reflexive, guttural 'tcch' and shook his head despairingly, just dramatically enough to be noticed as he stirred his coffee for at least the fifth time, not once looking up. Herman cut in, 'Yes, Luis, it's true that we've tried Agile but...'

'It doesn't work. It's shit.' Freddie butted in abruptly, addressing the room. 'Am I right? I'm right, aren't I? We all think that. We've all said it. It's shit. A complete waste of time. And money.' I didn't want Freddie to claim centre stage, so I immediately shot back with, 'Good. I'm glad you've said that,' hoping to wrongfoot him, 'and that's what I'm here to find out.'

'What? I just told you,' Freddie said, glaring at me, then at Herman.

'I need to know *why* it's shit. Why you think it's shit. That's all.'

Freddie laughed sarcastically, before adding, 'Look, I'm sorry Luka –'

'Luis,' Sabine corrected him, a line of annoyance crossing her brow.

'Luis,' Freddie continued, 'I don't mean to be rude…' – at which Christoph barely stifled a laugh. This seemed to irritate Freddie even further, who turned to him and said, 'No, Christoph, I won't have that. It's not that I'm being negative, but all of us around this table know that nothing that Herman's brought in has worked, quite frankly.'

'I'm not sure I agree with that,' Sabine interjected, 'and anyway, we haven't heard what Luis has to say. I, for one, would like to.'

There were general murmurs of consensus around the table and Freddie sat back and condescendingly waved an arm towards me to continue, 'have it your way'. I could see Herman bristle somewhat and I couldn't help wondering – is he a little scared of Freddie? If so, why? But there was no time to figure that out, at least not just yet. I held my composure and went in for the kill.

'You know, Friedrich, I actually don't disagree with you.' Now I had his attention. 'But it's not necessarily Agile itself that is "shit"; it's when it's not part of the long-term, ongoing strategy, and there are many, many reasons why often it doesn't feel right for an organisation. I get that. I've seen it many times. What I want to learn today is what your top-level experience has been like. Only then can I suggest a remedy. Is that OK?'

'Brilliant,' Leon chimed in. 'I've always thought we were doing something wrong, but I'm not the expert, so I wouldn't know what that was.'

'There have been hundreds of experts walk through that door,' Freddie countered, unhelpfully, 'and to what end? Nothing. Nada.'

'So tell me,' I entreated them all. 'What's the story?'

Sabine, who'd been listening to our exchanges quietly with a thoughtful expression, spoke in a measured, reflective tone, 'We're becoming too slow at what we do.'

'How so?' I asked, pleased that the discussion was finally moving on.

'Well, we're supposed to be this shit-hot digital era outfit, but our reach is actually very local. Germany, of course, then the Netherlands, Switzerland, a bit here and there in Belgium and maybe one or two scraps across Europe. But that's it.'

'Yeah,' said Christoph, 'and yet we have "International" as part of our name.'

'Strictly speaking, that is international,' Herman replied.

'But we're not truly international,' Christoph reminded them, 'and the way we're set up right now makes it hard to generate leads in the global marketplace if we can't release software faster.'

'I agree,' Sabine said, 'but how can we change? Because right now we're very project oriented.'

'Because that's how we do things. It's the way it's always been,' Freddie cut in.

'Exactly,' Sabine fired back, 'and what happens? Every time we try to create or launch something new, we spend nearly all our time sitting around this table arguing with each other, tying ourselves up in knots, red tape and bureaucracy.'

'Yeah,' Jonas added, 'I've lost count of the times my people have been assigned across multiple projects only to see them burn out or fall to pieces. There's not one team I haven't seen be broken by it all.'

'I'm sorry. I had no idea that was happening on a large scale. I've seen it happen once or twice, but I'm shocked, truly.' Herman appeared to be genuinely taken by surprise at this revelation.

'People are scared to speak up, that's why, because "it's the way we do things", isn't it?' Jonas said, looking at Freddie, who just shrugged.

'That's not my vision for this company, never has been,' Herman argued. 'I want us all to be working toward the same goal, not destroying people in the process. That's one of the reasons I invited Luis here today, because whatever it is we need to do, it must involve some sort of fundamental change.'

'Agreed,' said Christoph. 'The question is, how can we change what we're already doing when nothing so far seems to have worked? In that respect, I do have to agree with Freddie.'

Freddie allowed himself a not so well-hidden smirk of triumph, as if he was completely vindicated. In truth, I agreed with him more than he realised, but it was clear that Freddie seemed content to keep both feet firmly in the status quo, whereas at least Christoph and his colleagues appeared open to new ideas. They were all frustrated by their lack of progress, and even more concerned that if the trend continued, then potentially within eighteen months none of them would be sitting around this boardroom table.

Leon interjected, 'I think what I'd like to be confident in is knowing how we can connect our company strategy to the daily operations so that everyone understands how we can include some much-needed innovation in a way that's easy to implement.'

'And can we guarantee that this will have a positive impact on the business?' Sabine asked. 'It just seems like much of what we currently do is for the sake of it, or simply because we see a competitor launching something new and then try to emulate it.'

'Which doesn't necessarily bring in any extra business,' Christoph observed, 'in which case, there's little or no impact whatsoever. It seems to me we've lost sight of what it is our customers want from us in terms of the applications we already offer.'

'I think you're right,' Sabine agreed, 'we need to find ways of better understanding how we can utilise this huge mass of data we gather and then how we can generate meaningful insights based on our customers' behaviour. I mean, it must be sitting there already inside our software.'

Freddie frowned. IT was his domain, and he didn't look like he welcomed any outside criticism, no matter how well intended. Sabine continued, 'Do we even have a proper business model to respond to the digital era that is fit for purpose and could help us go global? I don't think so, but what would I know?'

It was a sobering moment. A heavy silence fell over all of them, even Freddie, although he seemed more interested in picking at his fingernails.

I'd been jotting down notes as they'd opened up, and I was pleased that they'd managed to articulate their concerns and not been afraid to admit that they didn't have the answers. In many ways, it was a moment of catharsis, delivered in a short burst of pent-up frustrations, underpinned by a willingness to drive forward toward a solution. Except for Freddie, which was interesting to observe. He seemed the eldest of the executive team, which didn't suggest to me that he was in any way a dinosaur – after all, he had partnered with Herman from the beginning and had very much been part of the early digital revolution. Yet he hadn't kept pace with the times. True, FSS's products were based on digital platforms, but the world of digital had moved on at a far greater pace than FSS had acknowledged. As a result, everyone in the room was stuck, not just because of the lack of digital innovation, but, as was becoming clear to me, because of the organisation's infrastructure. At least Herman had experienced some form of epiphany when he came across my blog about my ADAPT Methodology™ and had been triggered to reach out and seek my advice.

In my line of work, all too frequently I encounter organisations that become aware of the digital reality they find themselves operating in but have failed to keep pace with. Many of them will have implemented some form of Agile that ultimately hasn't delivered the desired results because they haven't embedded it as part of their organisational structure. The result is that they end up treading water, waiting to run out of energy, then sink because their current model is unsustainable in the face of leaner, more agile and adept competitors. Fear creeps into the boardroom and gradually leaks into the workforce.

I saw that fear behind Herman's gaze when he turned to me and asked, 'How can we start to make a change? What would be your approach?'

The proposal

As a non-traditional consultant, my approach is always the same: I begin with a pilot in just one part of the company. There's no point in trying to change the world in one go because it will always end in disaster. (I've seen it happen so many times in organisations that throw everything at the wall in the hope that something sticks.) There's nothing to be gained by trying to change everything at once because nothing will change. I strongly suspected that that's why FSS has remained where it was. Stuck.

Addressing the room, I explained that for change to happen it would require a shift in their mindset and practice, so that they focused on product and not projects. I could sense some confusion on their faces (except Freddie, now doodling on a notepad). I elaborated, explaining that each product needed its own business model. The product should be the primary focus and viewed in its entirety, beginning by defining the avatar (ie, the customer), identifying their pains and what problems the product would solve. Moving on, they would define the OKRs (objective key results), which would provide the essential framework for the vision to be achieved within three to five years, allowing them to translate strategy into operations.

This, in turn, would define the structure and skill set of the entire company required to release that product. They would then create a kind of start-up within the company centred around that product with the skill set that had been identified as necessary to deliver it. The key thing would be that product discovery would now always be integrated with product development.

'Of course, product is nothing without sales and so the ADAPT Methodology™ also pays particular attention to generating and maintaining strong lead funnels, through the Approach pillar,' I explained to the room.

'Sabine, you've been doing it all wrong, no wonder we only have a multimillion-euro turnover,' Freddie remarked.

'Not at all,' I replied, 'but knowing how to sell digital product more effectively in the digital marketplace will only strengthen your results in the long term. So many companies assume they're fully digital when, in fact, their sales operations resemble more traditional methods. When you add in the knowledge from the Data pillar, you then create a remarkable lead-to-sales funnel that keeps delivering.'

'That all sounds great, at least in principle,' Herman said, 'but how the hell do we know where to start?'

'You're right, it's a lot – too much – to take in without fully understanding what to expect from this type of transformation – because that's exactly what we're talking about here. Transforming your business so that it's fit for the digital era. The only way that will succeed is if you know what lies ahead.'

'More bullshit, I imagine,' said Freddie, standing up as if to leave.

'No. Wait. At least do Luis the courtesy of hearing him out,' Herman said firmly. Reluctantly, Freddie sat down.

'I get it,' I said. 'I know these last few months have given you all much cause for concern. And I agree, Friedrich, what's gone before doesn't seem to have done the trick. Part of my aim here today is to manage those expectations going forward.'

'How, exactly?' Freddie grunted.

'If you try to achieve this without some kind of roadmap, then believe me, you'll get lost. I want to invite you to a three-day workshop where I can introduce theoretical concepts and definitions that will enable you to create your own knowledge bank. I'll teach you how to approach new and existing customers in the digital era by utilising all the available digital data science tools to help you identify customer behaviour and generate insights. You'll also learn the fundamental essentials of Agility and subsequent digital product strategies that will allow you to harness their power and set in motion the transformation of this organisation. My hope is that we'll then work together to build a prototype specific to your business so that you can begin to apply the theory based on what your business does.'

'Basically, we'll learn what we need to do and why, and you'll tell us how,' Sabine remarked.

'Exactly,' I concurred, 'then down the line, if you need me to show you the how, we can think about a more hands-on approach.'

'You'd consult for us?' Herman asked.

'Of course,' I replied. Freddie looked unimpressed.

The morning had gone pretty much as I'd expected, albeit with a pocket of resistance (Freddie). The others seemed curious, enthusiastic and willing to embark on the three-day workshop. As Herman escorted me back down to reception, I sensed his demeanour was already a little lighter, and his eyes were shining.

'Brilliant, we'll set that workshop up,' he beamed. 'I'm curious. I really want this to work. I've spent so many years building this company, I've invested nearly all my time and energy into it, so there's no doubt I want this to work. Not just for me, but for everyone here so we can continue serving our customers, old and new.' He once again shook me firmly by the hand and patted me on the shoulder, confirming that his PA, Sonia, would be in touch with some suggested dates for the workshop.

By the time I was checking in for my return flight to Munich, Sonia's email pinged on my mobile.

THE ADAPT METHODOLOGY™
PROJECT TO PRODUCT SCORECARD

One session completed. Evaluate whether you are leading an outdated project-centric business or a modern product-led company at: https://bit.ly/Scorecard_ProductFirst_Book

2
Approach

I returned to Berlin three weeks later and checked into my hotel, only a short taxi ride from Adlershof Science Park. The following day's workshops were scheduled to start at 8am. The morning itself brought bright sunshine and clear blue skies, setting the scene – it was, I hoped, a good omen. Although luck rarely plays a part in business success; without a strategic plan to sustain it, fortunes are lost just as quickly as they're made.

By 7.30am I was unpacking my bag of tricks in FSS's conference room when Herman poked his head around the door, a look of eager anticipation on his face. His mood was as bright as the weather outside as he asked if he could have a quick word. 'Sure,' I said, without hesitation. Stepping fully into the room, Herman suddenly seemed a little anxious, though he was smiling, and asked if I'd give him a heads-up on what to expect from the first four-hour workshop. I respected the fact that he was keen to engage with what was about to unfold. It was the perfect mindset and completely in sync with the purpose behind the next three days. I wanted to feel confident that the CEO himself was ready to commit to some pretty intense discoveries with a view to taking away key learnings that he could then lead by example on, even though he wouldn't be on the front line of implementation. So far, Herman was meeting my expectations.

While pairing my laptop with the audio-visual equipment and setting up a good old-fashioned flipchart, I explained briefly that over the course of the morning I'd be pushing him and his colleagues to engage with dynamic thinking, as fast-paced as the digital landscape itself, as part of the Approach pillar. I said I'd elaborate further during the workshop, but that I would be steering them towards reaching three outcomes:

1. Identification of the avatar

2. Greater awareness of the nuanced ecology their business operated in

3. Heightened engagement with their customers

'Wow,' Herman said, 'all that in four hours?'

'Don't worry,' I smiled, 'once we get going, there will be no stopping you. Trust me.'

Herman nodded, satisfied that he knew the general direction of travel, though I hadn't given him any advantage over his colleagues before they arrived because I needed him to be mentally present to discover as much as he could for himself without being handed it on a plate. Any learnings he was about to make would be vital when evaluating where the business began, where it was now and, more significantly, where it could go in the future. He needed to feel as invested in the workshop as anyone else if he was to extract its maximum value.

Day One

Just before 8.00am, once the coffee and snacks had been laid out, Sabine and Christoph breezed in, deep in animated conversation about a news story they'd just heard about a competitor's significant uplift in sales.

'Is that what we're heading for, Luis?' Sabine laughed.

'That's the plan,' I said, returning her warmth.

'I don't know how they did it, but their entry into Scandinavia seems to really be paying dividends,' Christoph remarked.

We were joined by Leon and Jonas. Jonas, catching the tail end of the conversation, said assertively, 'I'm pretty sure it's not beyond us. We've spent millions over the last ten years on developing new projects.

I guess it's up to Freddie to let us know if our IT has the capacity.'

'Hopefully, that'll be one of the nuts we'll crack over these next three days,' I said, just as Herman returned to the room.

'No sign of Freddie?' Herman asked, looking quizzically at his team.

'He's probably just running late,' Sabine sighed, not convincing anyone.

'Not like him,' Herman pursed his lips. 'But, Luis, since most of us are here and I'm keen to make a start, let's crack on.'

'Ready when you are,' I replied. 'Good morning, everyone, welcome.' I began by explaining that the Approach workshop was based on the first of the five pillars of the ADAPT Methodology™:

1. Approach

2. Data

3. Agility

4. Product strategy

5. Transformation

With this first pillar, my aim was to teach them how to approach digital customers to generate leads, build a sales pipeline and, of course, sell more product in a global market and digital age – just as the competitor they'd been discussing had done.

At this point, Freddie entered the room, his phone clapped to his ear finishing off a call as he pulled out a seat and sat down. Meeting my gaze, he quipped, 'Did I miss anything important?'

Herman, irked, snapped, 'Freddie, we said 8 o'clock.'

'I'm here, aren't I? Sorry, have we solved the world's problems already? No offence, Luis.'

Leon tutted, irritated.

Despite Freddie's half-hearted apology, no offence was taken. I've come across many Freddies in my career, and I almost expect there to be at least one at the table. In some ways, I understand where people like Freddie are coming from, frustrating as it is to have to navigate their insecurities. For whatever reason, they feel threatened by being exposed to a world beyond their own lived experience. People like Freddie should never feel threatened by my workshops. The process is not about trying to remove their authority, or to make them feel redundant in any way. In reality, the biggest threat they face is the one they pose to themselves. As we progress through the workshop, I hope to show them that its intent is the opposite to what they imagined; rather than taking away their position, their authority and position within the business is enhanced. At this stage, though, I can't tell them that – and if I did, I probably wouldn't be believed. I need them to work it out for themselves.

As a matter of courtesy, I briefly recapped the purpose of the workshops to get Freddie up to speed.

'Huh. I didn't miss anything, then,' Freddie summarised inelegantly, but reading the room's disapproval, he passed his flippancy off as a joke. Nobody was laughing, but I smiled warmly to lift the mood.

'It's good to have you here,' I told him. 'Your IT insights and expertise will be invaluable.' I was being genuine, although I caught Leon repressing a smirk. It was interesting to see the executive dynamics at play so early in the first session. I moved swiftly on.

'This morning, while we're all feeling fresh, we're going to brainstorm how you approach your customers, how you reach them and grab their attention, turn them into leads and convert them to sales.'

'Can I just stop you for a moment?' Christoph interrupted. 'That's easy. We rarely, if ever, do any form of traditional marketing.'

'You mean like buying advertising space in print or online, no TV, no mass media?' I clarified.

'That's right,' Christoph confirmed. 'We mainly rely on referrals, or we pick up customers via the various network partners we've established relationships with over the years. That's worked well for us in building our database.'

'Until now?' I asked.

'Sure, things have plateaued, but that's because we have more competitors than ever before, so attrition is bound to happen.'

'Maybe so, but is that sustainable as a model? Especially if, as Herman has told me, your goal is to scale internationally.'

'Isn't that why you're here?' Freddie asked me, smirking.

'It is,' I confirmed. 'You may think that because you deliver your products via digital platforms that you're a digital organisation, but what I want to discover is if that's fit for the digital age when there are different approaches that could maximise your efforts. Perhaps, as things stand, your business model for growth just doesn't stack up.'

'What are we doing wrong?' Christoph asked. 'What's stopping us from reaching the mass market and going global? After all, that's what we're trying to do, and all our current customers seem to love our products.'

'I'm not disputing that. What is it that they love about your products?'

'The fact we offer customisation to meet their needs,' Sabine suggested.

'So you have a core range of products, but each customer tells you exactly what they want and you then tailor it to suit? Like a bespoke service?' I asked.

'Yes. That's always been our differentiator,' she confirmed.

'I told you this would be a waste of time,' Freddie muttered, leaning back in his chair. 'We've identified our niche, our partners they tell us what their customers want, we adapt, as you seem so keen on telling us to do, and voila – job done,' he said, snapping his fingers emphatically.

I wasn't going to be riled. 'You've obviously spent a lot of time and money developing these partnership relationships and releasing bespoke versions of your core software, but Herman's made it clear that things have changed. Sales aren't as robust as they once were, and this downward trend is having a negative impact on the company's ambition to go global.'

'That's right,' Herman agreed.

'Doesn't that suggest that either your network partners and their customers are wanting something different, or that market conditions have changed?' I challenged them.

'Or both?' Jonas suggested. Freddie closed his eyes and slumped further into his chair, looking as if he couldn't take any more. I'm not sure he would have been subjected to a workshop like this in his petrochemical career.

'Which suggests you need to find ways to create a brand that will appeal to those new customers beyond your existing market share and then create awareness of it to attract the necessary engagement. To do that, you need to acknowledge that what's missing right now is an effective digital strategy to enter those new markets and inspire, particularly in the US, then all the other major English-speaking economies. Right now, you have to admit, you're just treading water,' I told them.

'Oh, please.' Freddie countered, suddenly sitting up straight, more alert than he'd been all morning. 'Herman, tell him. I've worked at a very senior level for one of the biggest industrial manufacturers in Germany. I understand business; I know it inside out. That's why you hired me, isn't it? Because I know how these things work.' Freddie was looking quite agitated and flushed.

'Nobody here's disputing that,' Herman assured him.

'Really?' Freddie spat back. 'Don't forget, I've been here from the beginning, right behind you, supporting you at every turn, on every whim. There's nothing wrong with our products and the way we do things here. Every business has peaks and troughs, just like the stock markets, and just like them we'll bounce back, mark my words. There are plenty of people out there who'd love to get results like our 55-million-euro turnover last year.'

'But this business is no longer growing,' I stated simply.

'No, it's not, but that's purely down to lack of resources – as I've been banging on about, Herman,' Freddie shot back.

Herman looked surprised at being singled out so publicly, but Freddie gave him no room to respond and continued, 'If you're serious about growth, we need to face facts: we don't have enough people in development, we've got no real budget to hire the right people and we're over-subscribed as it is. Why we're even thinking about going global when we're doing OK just as we are is beyond me.'

'Because "doing OK" isn't enough. The numbers – not ours, but our competitors' – speak for themselves,' Herman steamed.

'Then maybe Sabine here should get off her backside and sell more product,' Freddie glared.

'Enough, Friedrich. I won't have us reduced to a petty blame culture. There's too much at stake here, for all of us, including you.'

Freddie seemed taken aback by Herman's sudden vehemence. Though as I mentioned, bubbles always burst. Sabine, still smarting from Freddie's personal criticism, slapped both palms down on the table and said firmly, 'We've got to do something. I'm with Herman on this. If we carry on as we are for the next five years, I can't see a long-term future for us. We've got competitors cropping up all over the place, not just here in Germany, but all over Europe. We can no longer claim to have an edge. We don't even have a plan to penetrate new markets, and even if we did, we don't know who our potential customers are, let alone how to reach them. We just don't have the networks.'

The room fell silent. Sabine had hit the nail on the head and so I waited to see how this would diffuse. It was Freddie who broke the team's awkward silence when he proffered a (small) olive branch: 'Like I said, we're doing OK but maybe we'll strike lucky and get a referral from an English-speaking customer at some point.'

'Thank you, Freddie,' Herman replied, his tone more conciliatory, adding, 'but we need more than just a "maybe" if we want to thrive in the not-so-distant future. Even though our affiliates and partners seem perfectly happy with how we customise our products for them, we need a clear plan and, as yet, we don't have one that guarantees our future growth.'

'Are you saying we should just kill that side of the business and what we're good at and start over from scratch?' Freddie asked.

'Not at all,' Herman replied. 'That would be suicide. That's what's keeping us afloat and we've all done exceptionally well with it. I congratulate the whole company in that respect. The reality is, though, the market – our market – is shifting, and I'm not sure we have the tools to adjust. At present, we're standing still and being outperformed by disruptive competitors.'

'Herman's right,' Sabine said, and then, looking at Freddie, added, 'and even you know it.'

'We need to find ways of investing what we can into sponsoring a new business model,' Herman urged.

'This is good,' I interrupted. 'Herman clearly has a vision for where he believes the business should be heading.'

'Yes, I do,' he agreed. 'We want to scale by targeting a global market, but I think we need to recognise that this means our customers will change too. Our focus won't be solely on corporate clients, but also on the small traders and growing army of individual freelancers.'

'And to make that vision a reality, the business needs to adapt, not simply adjust,' I observed. 'That may mean releasing fewer customised products that are expensive to create, and instead offering an alternative, single solution. The question is: who is your target avatar and what would that offering look like?'

'That's going to be one hell of an overhaul,' observed Jonas, with his operations and quality assurance hats on.

'Go on,' I invited him.

'It means creating a whole new product, from the ground up. That's a lot of extra work if we don't have the right resources in place.' Leon looked to his colleagues for agreement, though not everyone seemed to share his view.

'Hang on,' Jonas chipped in, 'let's look at what we do now. For a large proportion of our customers we find ways of incrementing features to customise the product, but because that results in a bespoke version tailored to their invoicing needs, it isn't appropriate for others. So we end up with thousands of different customisations that provide thousands of different solutions. Leon, that sounds like an operational nightmare.'

The room burst into spontaneous laughter as everyone recognised the truth in what Jonas was saying. He continued, more seriously, 'I'm coming around to your thinking, Herman, that if we want to go global and target a different customer base as the market evolves, that model is unsustainable.'

In summary of the discussion so far, I reflected to them their collective thoughts:

- Herman wanted to enter the global marketplace.

- The team realised the company lacked an effective product strategy to achieve that.

Freddie remained sceptical, hostile even, and so there wasn't total consensus, but the majority were with me and willing to think about the gateway to enter that new market. It would require them to execute a completely different business model, following the principles set out in the Approach pillar, which dives deep into articulating strategy and defining an avatar.

Strategy

The first thing I wanted them to address was defining their avatar. On the flipchart, I wrote the following five basic questions, asking, 'What's the strategy…'

- For your content, to approach and appeal to customers?

- To create awareness among those customers?

- To generate leads through content creation?

- To engage with customers?

- To generate leads and close sales?

I asked them to, for the next thirty minutes, think about who they believed their dream customer would be, that would generate sales in the new business arena they wanted to enter. 'Remember,' I said, 'this isn't your current customer avatar, it's the one you want to target with your new product, utilising your new business model. This is probably the most crucial exercise you'll do, because your entire product strategy will centre around this avatar.'

I prompted them to think deeply about this, writing some additional prompts on the flipchart:

- What gender are they?

- What's their name?

- What age range do they fall into?

- What's their marital status?

- What's their job?

- Which social media platforms do they use?

I reminded them, 'The time you spend defining these characteristics will determine everything going forward, so take your time and consider them carefully.'

Within fifteen minutes, they'd agreed that their avatar was:

- Female

- Called Jessica

- Aged thirty-seven

- Co-habiting

- A freelance graphic designer based in the USA with a large portfolio of clients

- A user of LinkedIn, Instagram, Twitter and Facebook (in that order of preference)

They explained that their gender choice was based on surveys that showed a narrow split in favour of females, despite Freddie's protests that 'most graphic designers I know are men,' quickly shot down by Sabine. It was this old-fashioned thinking that once prevented women like her from ever making it to board level. 'It's called "unconscious bias", Freddie,' she reminded him, much to Herman's amusement.

Next, I invited them to consider:

- What pains and frustrations does Jessica currently experience when invoicing her clients?

- What does she ideally want her invoicing software to deliver?

- How does she suffer by using your competitor's software?

- What advantages would she gain from switching to FSS's product?

In the discussion that followed, the team exchanged various opinions and perspectives as they engaged with this first pillar of the roadmap.

'When we go global our customer base will definitely change,' Sabine noted.

'So will the customer profile,' added Christoph.

'Why?' Freddie challenged.

Sabine, exasperated, replied, 'Because freelancers' needs are different to those of corporate clients.'

'So, what? We can customise, like we always do.'

'But Freddie, that's time-consuming and expensive,' Jonas interjected, 'and it always takes so long to agree anything. My team once had to wait five weeks to get a sign off, and not without a lot of disagreement over something trivial. We lost the client because they ran out of patience with all the delays.'

'Who didn't sign it off in time?' Herman asked.

'It was you, actually,' Jonas said, awkwardly, 'but to be fair, it was because we got held up by quality assurance when the project manager was off sick for three weeks and then you were on holiday.'

'Also,' Leon interjected, 'with so many customisations, it can be confusing. It's hard to keep track.'

Freddie looked sceptical, 'Rubbish. How do you think we got to number one in Germany if it was so difficult?'

Herman shut him down, 'Except when we enter a new market, we'll be an unknown entity. We'll not be number one then.'

'That's Christoph's department,' said Freddie, sullenly.

'Only if we know who we're targeting and are clear on what it is they need from us,' Christoph defended.

But Freddie wasn't put off. 'Simple: invoicing software solutions that make their lives easier and brings in the cash on time to pay their bills.'

'There's a big difference between the needs of one person working on their own and a corporate giant with huge cash reserves behind them. We can't rely on our current customer profiles when we go in a new direction,' Sabine countered.

'Exactly,' said Christoph, looking vindicated.

At this point, Herman interjected, returning to the task. 'So, what's our avatar – Jessica – looking for?'

'A one-stop software solution that can produce everything she needs with optional premium add-ons, should she ever want to upgrade,' Sabine said.

'On an ad-hoc basis?' asked Christoph.

'Or maybe subscription-based,' she suggested.

'Stored on a secure cloud, with twenty-four-seven access,' Leon added.

Jonas was looking interested now too. 'With a real-time currency converter depending on which territory she's billing, but which also allows her to be paid in her home currency.'

'Yes,' agreed Christoph, 'and it would be locally tax-compliant, updating automatically when rates change.'

'And aligned to any local reporting variations in whichever territory the invoice lands,' Leon added.

'Which tracks her clients' custom regularity and automatically applies any agreed volume discounts,' said Sabine, looking excited.

'Could it have AI-generated reminders, set according to parameters, that act as her credit control?' Jonas suggested.

Christoph nodded, 'And how about a colour-coded dashboard that shows which clients she's not invoiced for a while, or which sends a personalised reach-out to generate a response?'

Freddie still looked unimpressed. 'Oh, please, just get yourself a virtual PA. Besides, some of this we do already.'

'Agreed,' said Jonas. 'No need to completely reinvent the wheel. Right now, we offer this bespoke service on demand, no two products are the same. What if we could offer all these premium add-ons as standard, so that the customer simply selects them as and when they're needed? That would reduce our cost of doing business significantly.'

Herman nodded enthusiastically, 'And we could redeploy those savings to other areas, or feed them back into the P&L.'

'Aha,' Freddie interrupted, 'so we're going to make people redundant, that's what this is all about – I knew it.'

They all turned toward me, looking for an answer. I made eye contact with each of them as I replied, 'That all depends on where your operational priorities lie. At this moment, that's yet to be decided. By you.'

The flow of conversation in the room was heated, exciting and exhilarating. Despite Freddie constantly throwing up barriers and his grudging acceptance of the majority's desire to pursue this line of enquiry, this was valuable insight into FSS's development process.

I'd asked them to step into a new customer's shoes, something that, as a business, they'd been backing away from, becoming complacent following years of success. While their heads had been buried in the sand, the world around them had moved on. I was challenging them to view their business objectively and to ask themselves how their offering and targeting needed to change within the new global context. For the first time, they'd been prompted to examine how they might then deliver on that in terms of product, as opposed to a project – although at this stage they weren't aware that this was the direction they were being steered toward. That would all become clear in the Product pillar when they'd realise that their options to scale become far greater on a product-led rather than project-led approach.

Like many businesses founded on traditional principles, their current modus operandi was dictated by the demands of individual departmental silos, which fosters in-fighting and politicking, creating rabbit holes and barriers. That set up is not conducive to developing a product for specific clients. Nor is it an ideal way to structure an organisation fit for the digital era.

I was pleased: their initial progress had been immense. They had defined their avatar and I'd sown the seeds for thinking more about being product-led, and not project-led. We stopped for a well-earned break.

Awareness

Refreshed and inspired by the first discussion, after a ten-minute break I turned their attention back to their avatar and how to raise awareness to, ultimately, generate sales via the top, middle and bottom layers of the sales funnel.

Free-to-access product content.

No contact details requested.

Request prospect's contact details (email address/phone number/job title) in order to access further information.

Provide a product demo that fully engages prospect and encourages a call to action to take the next step.

Sales Funnel

'You've done some great work identifying your avatar – I congratulate you. I want you to build on that and think about what kind of content you could create related to the product to persuade them to respond to the call to action. Try to avoid the typical lesson-learning blogs and the inevitable digital download. That's an old-hat marketing tool; people have cottoned on and turned off.'

Sabine immediately jumps in with, 'I love a good podcast. I listen to them on the U-Bahn on my way to work.'

'What gets your attention?' I asked, pleased that she was on the same page already.

'Anything that will improve my leadership skills.'

'And…?' I press her.

'Actually, I've picked up some useful tips and put them into action.'

'Great. What about our avatar? What might be of interest to her?'

'How to negotiate the best rates?' Christoph suggested.

'Nurturing great relationships with your clients so that invoicing will be hassle-free,' Leon added. 'It must be difficult for freelancers, especially when they start out.'

'The "invoice to payment" digitisation journey,' Jonas offered. 'That could be interesting.'

'Excellent, and any of those topics can be repurposed in blogs, videos, articles, etc, because each help to raise awareness of both your brand and your product to a target market without any initial commitment on their part. That's the top of the funnel,' I explained.

'It's expensive,' Freddie observed. 'It uses up a load of resources we need elsewhere. Who pays for all that free stuff? Are you happy to take that out of your budget, Sabine?' he asked.

'Actually, that's a good question, Freddie,' I smiled. 'But just as Herman observed earlier, when your operation becomes leaner, redeploying budget from one money-hungry unit to another is a good investment if there's a strategic plan in place designed to speed up the ROI. I'll return to that later.'

'It's coming my way, then,' Christoph joked, punching the air, much to the amusement of the room.

I then highlighted the middle segment of the sales funnel. 'Here, unlike the top of the funnel, we're asking for some basic contact details in return for downloading targeted free content.' Again, I turned to the room for their suggestions on what that might be.

'I do this all the time,' Herman said. 'The last one was on Sunday, a whitepaper on the five steps to AI success. And of course, Luis, content from your website, too.'

'A webinar could be instructive for freelancers,' Christoph said, his enthusiasm rising as the thought took hold, 'especially if digital invoicing was new to them. We could walk them through the product, subscription packages and answer any questions, either in real time via chat, or by email. We've got some bright graduates in marketing who would probably love to get their teeth into this.'

'We're always being invited to complete scorecards by tech industry suppliers wanting us to sign up to them,' Jonas offered, 'maybe that's something we could adopt, too, for freelancers. Something along the lines of measuring their invoicing-to-payment ratios.'

'Again, great, interesting suggestions,' I said. 'The key is knowing your avatar's pain inside out and offering them useful, targeted content that they're willing to part with their contact details for in return. At which point, you've captured a prospect's data, with consent, and you know that they're aware of you.'

Moving down to the bottom level, I again opened the floor to the team. They could see the words 'free demo' and I wanted to know their initial thoughts.

'Could we run some type of mini course on finance and accounting for new freelancers?' suggested Sabine.

'I don't see why not,' Herman mused.

'Why? What's in it for us?' Freddie countered.

'A free trial of the product,' Christoph fired back. 'Simple.' It wasn't clear if he was answering the question or critiquing Freddie's attitude and I filled the uncertain pause quickly: 'As a call to action, one of the most effective ways to help convert a prospect to a customer is by inviting them on an integrated journey that offers them free-to-access, real-value content, resulting in a verified reason to purchase. But when raising awareness, you need to cover all your bases. Where will your avatar stumble across your product? Go back to your avatar profile – you identified that LinkedIn was her first choice of social media platform, but think about that carefully. Is that where she markets her own content for B2B consumption? Does she turn to other platforms to consume content herself?'

'We need to figure out the strategy for advertising the top of the funnel,' Christoph said. 'For example, do we advertise the podcasts? The same with blogs and videos. And how often?'

'I think Jessica would use Instagram, in that case,' Sabine said, 'but we could do some research on that. Maybe that's where we begin to raise awareness.'

'By pushing our content or placing straightforward ads,' Christoph suggested.

'Maybe we use different channels in different parts of the funnel and tailor the offering in each,' Leon added.

'We'd also need to work out where take-up of blogs and videos is highest. Is that LinkedIn, Twitter? I don't know,' Herman said. 'I bet our millennial colleagues could help us out there.'

'When you do your research,' I cautioned, 'keep your avatar profile front of mind and remember, it's their shoes you're walking in.'

Leads

With their attention firmly on how to raise awareness, I segued swiftly onto how to get leads. Having considered the ways in which to place and target various content offers, I wanted the executive team to drill down further now that they could see they had digitally led options for driving traffic.

I opened this section with, 'You've considered ways to target, now we need to retarget. The question is: what do you want to retarget, and how do you create lead magnets?'

'Do you mean that a podcast could relate to, for example, a mini accounting course, so that one part of the funnel leads directly to the call to action in the bottom segment?' Herman asked.

'Exactly,' I confirmed.

'Presumably, then, we could introduce in the top segment that we've created a PDF download to encourage them to cascade to the middle where it will convert into some basic contact information?' Christoph said.

'That's one way of acquiring leads, yes,' I agreed. 'The second approach is to capture email details by advertising, for example, a webinar about personal accounting.'

'Why on earth would we want to do that?' Freddie sounded exasperated.

'Webinars generate hotter leads. People who sign up are generally very interested in the subject matter so are more likely to be attentive and open to what you're presenting to them. It's an ideal opportunity to position yourself as an expert and demonstrate your expertise and product efficacy, important factors when prospects are selecting a supplier. It's also great for showing your personality and tone of voice, indicating whether you are a brand that's easy to engage with.'

'So, this is all just about the hard sell. We're making ourselves look desperate,' Freddie said.

'I don't think so,' Leon interjected. 'This sounds like a much more subtle and nuanced approach,' to which I added, 'Anything that comes across as too pushy or jargon-heavy will turn potential customers off.'

'In that case, I guess we won't be asking Freddie to front any of our podcasts,' Sabine joked. Freddie didn't seem to appreciate the joke. Fortunately, we were ready to take another short break.

Engagement

When the team returned from their break, I wrote on the flipchart the following numbers: 7–12–4.

This was met with blank faces all round. I explained that engagement in the digital era is a science, and is effectively activated through:

- Seven hours of content
- With twelve touchpoints
- Via four different channels

'The aim for the next thirty minutes is to design an engagement strategy that follows this pattern so that by the time we progress to the last session on sales, we know how to close the deal.'

I could already see Christoph scribbling furiously on his jotter pad. He seemed to have understood what we'd been discussing so I was happy for him to take the initiative and lead. Marketing was his baby, after all. I invited him to write his ideas on the flipchart. Jumping from his seat, his enthusiasm was infectious and captured his colleagues' attention immediately. He started to write, frequently turning from the chart to his colleagues, wanting to ensure he had their full attention.

'Okay,' he began. 'When we publish a blog post, that's the first touchpoint. We can use various internet and social media channels for the purpose of retargeting, and we could include an email for one of our sales reps. Better still, if a prospect subscribes to receive a free mini accounting course here at the bottom of the funnel, that creates chances for several more interactions too. If, after two weeks, the prospect hasn't converted to a sale, somebody from our team can make a strategic call to offer a place in an online workshop. Or we could point them in the direction of more in-depth video content that we think would engage them – based on knowing our avatar inside out – so that achieves those seven hours of viewable content. In doing so, we're reinforcing our brand, our expertise and our product, in line with the 7–12–4 principle.'

Observing Christoph's mind-mapping on the flipchart was like watching the creation of an abstract artwork. As he added his next flourish, an audible sigh from Freddie prompted him to pause.

'Freddie, I know what you're thinking –' (Freddie's raised eyebrow indicated that he doubted this) '– that seven hours of content is too much of an ask for anyone to create, let alone engage with. But think about it, Sabine told us she loves to listen to podcasts on her way into the office. If she listens to five podcasts that last thirty minutes each, that's already two and a half hours. We just need to design a strategy that gets the balance right across all the content we'll create. If I understand Luis correctly, prospects will respond more favourably if they've consumed seven hours of content in various forms than they would to a call from a sales rep.'

'Why?' Freddie butted in.

'Because they need to establish in their mind that we're the authority and can solve their problem. It's about gaining their trust, isn't it?' Herman said.

'And by engaging them in these ways, we're able to address their concerns or questions through educating them,' Jonas added.

'You also inspire them, through your own evangelising,' I explained. 'This offers them valuable insights and draws them into your product, which encourages follow-through to a purchase.'

'I completely get it,' Christoph enthused, 'I hadn't seen before how this would all link together.'

'In that case,' I said, 'let's close the deal and move onto the final element of the Approach pillar – sales.'

Sales

The final sixty minutes on the first pillar, which is focused on sales, never fails to light up the room.

The usual perception is that if you can crack sales, all the other problems will disappear. To some extent, that is true. But sales are only one outcome of a bigger process and without a roadmap fit for the digital era, the opportunities to grow sales are often lost.

'Before you start, I have a question,' Freddie raised his hand, before leaning on his elbow and pointing at the flipchart that still displayed Christoph's mind map. 'I think we all know where this is going…'

From the others' expressions, I wasn't sure they agreed, but they waited for his question. 'You're either about to wave a magic wand or tell us how to suck eggs.'

'That's not a question,' Herman pointed out.

'No,' Freddie agreed, 'but I'm guessing the answer will be how the hell we should do sales, because for the last fifteen years we've been doing it all wrong. I'm right, aren't I?' He sucked his teeth and slouched back into his seat.

'Ah, so there's the question,' Herman said, not seeming pleased with Freddie's assumption. 'Luis, is he right? Are we doing sales wrong?' From his demeanour, I was pretty sure that Herman didn't share Freddie's dismissive attitude.

'I'd welcome the chance to hear what Freddie thinks, first. Freddie, do you mind?' I gestured for him to expand.

Freddie clearly didn't mind. He stood up and approached the flipchart, standing ready to deliver a lecture.

'We've obviously been doing it all wrong, haven't we? From a small start-up with limited capital behind us, to growing into a multimillion-euro enterprise with nearly a hundred people working here and hundreds of clients across Europe. Clearly, we've been making big mistakes.'

Freddie was enjoying his moment in the sun and, although I was pleased he had taken the reins, for now, I could sense several people in the room bristling.

'So now we need to adopt this great new plan Christoph has dreamt up –'

'It's not a plan, they're just ideas,' Christoph interjected.

Freddie ignored him and continued '– that requires us to spend hours and hours of time inventing... *content* – videos, more blogs and, wait for it, stuff to give away, for free. For free! That sounds like charity to me, not business. And what if, after all that time, effort and money spent producing all of this, it turns out nobody wants to sit through seven hours of *content?* What if they happen to like what we are already selling and, hey presto, they buy it? There you go, sales.'

Herman looked frustrated, 'Have you actually been listening this morning? You and I both know sales are flatlining.'

'It's a blip.'

'No, it's not a blip. We're at serious risk of decline, we're no longer number one.'

'We are in Germany. Oh, and Austria,' Freddie threw back at him.

'The figures speak for themselves. Our competition is biting at our ankles, even here at home, and you know that. You *must* know that?' Herman implored him.

Freddie continued to argue. 'We just need to redouble our efforts, that's all. Do what we're good at and do it better.'

'Is that your solution? Because, Freddie, I disagree with you.'

'Then we must agree to disagree,' Freddie said, returning to his seat.

'No, we won't,' Herman said emphatically. A palpable tension hung in the air. I let it hang for no longer than necessary.

'I want to thank you, Freddie,' I said, resuming control of the discussion, 'and, to be honest, some of what you say is correct.' Both Herman and Freddie seemed startled by my comment. 'If you'll allow me…' I took my place by the flipchart. 'Today, in the digital world, it's true, you don't need to wait for leads to consume a drip feed of 7 hours of content, and nor is it prescriptive. If they want it immediately, they can just buy.'

Freddie looked triumphant.

'However,' I warned, 'what I'm describing is a whole process that fully engages and draws people into your sales pipeline. That pipeline is a model, designed using software that can be re-run over and over again to reach the numbers you want, all over the world, linked into local sales teams and call centres. For example, in Asia, North America, Europe, wherever you want, they'll call hot leads across time zones that have engaged with your content via the 7–12–4 principle. That's how an integrated digital strategy will help your sales go global.'

'I agree,' Christoph said. 'If we ensure that everyone who engaged with the 7–12–4 ends up in the sales pipeline, our growth will be exponential.'

'Won't that be pretty labour intensive,' Leon asked, 'meaning there'll be extra overhead?' I shook my head and explained, 'You can easily build sales teams using freelancers found on networks such as Upwork or Fiverr. Just hook them up to local numbers in every territory you want to enter. They're the ones closing the deals and that's how you generate a global sales machine.'

'In any country?' Sabine asked.

'In any country. You follow the same process in the local language. That's exactly how my company, Evolution4all, was designed,' I told them.

'All pretty simple,' Freddie said, dismissively.

'Actually yes, it is,' I said. 'I'm not suggesting this won't take a lot of effort and real investment to make it work, but the process is simple. As long as you all buy into it, that is. There are four more pillars to follow, and each will build on the others so that you can follow the roadmap to creating an FSS for the digital era. The decisions you make based on this roadmap will become the plans you then put into action.' And with that, our first session was complete.

Four hours had flown by and it was time for lunch. The opening session is where I test the temperature of the executive team and its willingness (or not) to engage with my ideas. Freddie was not atypical in that respect, but I like to believe that my rationale will usually, at some point, get through. I was curious to see how the day would develop, given his reticence, but I was equally fascinated to see how the others had responded to this in positive ways that seemed to unlock their lateral thinking abilities. For many boards facing similar market threats, it's too easy to procrastinate and not make decisions, which only compounds their problems. My job is to bring new thinking, energy and inspiration to the table, which hopefully culminates in a laser-sharp focus that pinpoints the energy in the room, listening, responding and turning the room into a crucible of creativity. At the very least, this should generate a variety of opinions and suggestions specific to the needs of that business, which can then be developed into actionable plans.

At FSS, so far everything was progressing as expected. I'd seen how they could (mostly) coalesce around a single objective and work together in a way that perhaps they hadn't allowed themselves to for some time. Their biggest gains were in identifying their avatar and giving shape to a strategic plan that they could commit to with a good degree of confidence. Already I could sense the shift in their collective mindset, away from believing they were a digital business. The reality was, producing a huge range of customised digital products was proving to be an operational nightmare mired in the traditional silo structures of the twentieth century. But I could sense them adopting better group accountability. They seemed aware that the digital landscape had moved on and that they had a lot of catching up to do if they wanted to grow and enter new markets.

THE ADAPT METHODOLOGY™
PROJECT TO PRODUCT SCORECARD

Two sessions completed. Evaluate whether you are leading an outdated project-centric business or a modern product-led company at: https://bit.ly/Scorecard_ProductFirst_Book

3
Agility

You will notice that for the next part of the workshop I jump ahead to the third pillar, Agility, instead of the second, Data. My logic is that the 'D' for 'Data' in the ADAPT Methodology™ comes last because this is not a linear process; it's a composite, of which data is the final component. I also like to disrupt people's thinking. It's tempting to rush to the data when looking for answers to problems and concerns in a business, but that's not always the best place to start.

I begin by explaining that the term 'Agile' is often misunderstood, both in theoretical terms and in its implementation. Viewed by many as a panacea to problematic organisational thinking and operations, in practice the results are often below initial expectations, certainly in respect of the impact on the infrastructure. There are numerous reasons for this, principally the lack of executive buy-in and especially participation. This leaves the top layer disconnected from all the good work that Agile consultants and employees put into trying to make Agile effective. My aim is to connect those layers and enable a business to become a truly digital product organisation.

FSS's experience has, to date, been typical of traditionally structured companies where Agile has been shoe-horned in as a management-level process while never being fully embedded in its business philosophy. It doesn't surprise me to learn that, amongst most of the executive team, Herman included, disenchantment set in when Agile fell short of expectations. It was viewed as an expensive failure. Their critique showed exactly why they had evaluated it this way – the key indicator was their collective view of Agile as an 'exercise'.

Comparing Agile and Waterfall

All too often, the implementation of Agile lacks substance and meaning. For too long, FSS had relied heavily on Waterfall methodologies to develop and release software instead of creating the capacity to be Agile. This had seen the business invest heavily in new product software development over long periods of time, only to get underwhelming results when they were released to market. This, I knew, would be where Freddie and I were likely to butt heads the most. I was not interested in assigning blame because, truth be told, the whole executive team shared culpability for previous failures to realise the ROI they needed to grow. This workshop was designed to reset their thinking so that, going forward, they would be not only informed, but part of the implementation.

Shifting expectations is key to success, beginning with understanding the theories behind Agile that would show them how it could best be achieved when combined with the practical implementation of technical excellence through continuous delivery, the subject of the next session.

The lunch break had given everyone a much-needed energy boost. They'd been prompted to think in new ways about their overall approach toward customers in a digital landscape when they already believed they were a digitally driven company. I could see that their notepads were full of exclamation marks, arrows and doodles. When we were all gathered again, I felt like I had their full attention – with the exception of Freddie, who resumed his folded-arms position. I knew he would again be my toughest critic in the session to come.

I wrote on the flipchart: Agile – is it easier to understand than implement?

'Does anyone have a view on this?' I asked.

Freddie raised his hand. 'Complete waste of time. We engaged an Agile consultancy last year to "help" us with some software development, on Herman's insistence.'

'How did that go?' I asked, curious to hear more.

'I wouldn't say it was a complete waste of time,' Herman rebutted, 'it was an interesting exercise. And from what I heard, many in the IT team could see there were certain advantages to adopting leaner practices.'

'News to me,' Freddie chipped back, seeming irritated at having been contradicted.

'The word was that, on the whole, it seemed to work well, it just didn't go far enough,' Herman explained.

'Exactly,' Freddie was quick to agree, 'because it made no sense to the rest of the business, that's why. Same old arguments and same old problems. In the end, we didn't achieve anything except losing cash from our departmental budget, so we had to go crawling to finance when we needed to upgrade our servers.'

'Was Agile viewed principally as an IT department project?' I asked.

'Of course it was. It's always IT's area,' Freddie snapped.

'Have you reverted to Waterfall, in that case?'

'Yes,' Herman answered. 'That's what we use with every project we do, IT-related or otherwise.'

'But…?' I hinted.

'It's not a matter of finding fault, it's what we know,' Herman justified.

'And unlike Agile, it delivers,' Freddie snapped again.

'I wouldn't agree with that,' Jonas remarked. 'Yes, we've had our successes in the past where we've spent months developing a new product, rolling it out and seeing great take-up. But – and here's the "but" you're looking for Luis – more often than not we're behind the customer curve. One win is outweighed by two fails. In that respect, Waterfall drains our resources too.'

'And the resulting fallout between departments hasn't always been pleasant,' Leon commented, 'with sales blaming marketing, or ops having a go at IT. It causes a lot of bad feeling.'

'I completely get that,' I said. 'Actually, it's nobody's fault. I'm sure the Agile team you called in did exactly what was asked of them. I'm here to show you that there's another way and, once you understand how to employ the tools and maximise your individual skill sets, you'll view Agile in a new light. You'll also have the right information from the outset to see its implementation through successfully.'

'We'll see about that,' Freddie mumbled.

'So tell us, what's the solution?' Herman asked.

'Put simply, you need an integrated strategy that involves everyone who's needed to release a product to market. It's not confined to one department; it requires group thinking to implement it properly. Agile is a process that carries this through from beginning to end – except the ending is viewed through a different lens, determined by a whole set of cycles driven by rolling objective key results, or OKRs – I'll explain what those are later. For now, let me summarise where I believe FSS is currently.'

I began writing up bullet points on the flipchart. Essentially, they said that FSS lacked a consistent, integrated strategy. In terms of their product delivery, this was a time-consuming waste of resources and energy that led to backlogs and delays.

'This explains why the business is falling behind the customer curve,' Sabine observed.

I added that ultimately, this risked employee burnout and dissatisfaction. Who would feel motivated to get out of bed in the morning knowing the mountain they'd need to climb once they set foot through the door?

'Primarily, the dilemma you face is that, in today's world, a digitally led business that has both feet anchored in Waterfall is out of step. The traditional project-led philosophy simply isn't compatible with the need to deliver product that helps the business grow rapidly and scale toward a sustainable future. The reality is, you need to change. And change is –'

'Scary,' Christoph finished for me. They all nodded in agreement.

'The good news is,' I reassured them, 'for the most part, you likely already have the necessary skillsets under your roof; all you need are some tools to make change happen and be effective. This is where I can help. First, I want to share the theory behind Agile. Then I'll talk about the practicalities of implementing it, in the second half of this pillar, which focuses on continuous delivery. This is aimed at executive level because, as you know by now, without your commitment and involvement, implementation gets pushed down through the hierarchy, creating a disconnect that permeates the entire company. Any questions?'

Freddie raised his hand.

'I still don't see the point. Our products are digital. We deliver everything digitally; we've probably not produced any hard copy support material for ten years. We've been successful and have the revenue to prove that. My IT team is sprint-savvy and not one of us around this table doesn't have a LinkedIn account, so surely that makes us "digital"? My question, again, is why is it so important to have an Agile organisation? Why do we need to change?'

'What would Nokia say?' I countered.

'I don't know. What would Nokia say? They're irrelevant these days.'

'Exactly,' I reply. 'My best introduction to the need for Agility was when I worked for them, back in 2005 when they still dominated the mobile comms market. On the engineering side, they were the acknowledged leaders in their field, and they had the revenue to prove it. Much like you've described FSS's market position.'

'I'm not sure that's a fair comment,' Freddie grumbled, looking around the table for agreement. But Herman looked thoughtful and said, 'Let's hear him out.'

I continued, 'It was a lavish place to work: luxurious buildings and team facilities, a great culture. They were king of the world – until 2007 when Apple's iPhone hit the market. Even back then, when early iterations of the product first fell into customers' hands, it revolutionised the way people used mobile devices. It fed customers' needs, before they even knew what they were, and those needs then became standard requirements: complete connectivity through internet, email, cameras, business and consumer apps. Even in its formative era, customers couldn't get enough of Apple's innovation. Within three years, Nokia was almost completely wiped out. Imagine that: a behemoth practically obliterated by a disruptor competitor.'

I turned to write on the flipchart a quote from the great automobile industry innovator and business philosopher, W Edwards Deming, who moved to Japan post-World War Two to remodel Toyota's production system: 'It is not necessary to change. Survival is not mandatory.'[3]

'What Deming reminds us of is that no matter how huge an organisation becomes, that doesn't guarantee its longevity.'

I could see the colour start to drain from Herman's face.

'How does Apple's success link with Agile?' Leon asked. 'Surely it was just because they invented a product that took off?'

'Exactly,' Freddie agreed.

'That's interesting, so what do you think Nokia could have done to avoid their near total collapse?' I asked.

'Copy Apple, obviously,' Freddie replied, 'like the others that entered the market have done. We have imitators, too, you know.'

---

3   WE Deming, 'It is not necessary to change…' (The Deming Institute, no date), https://deming.org/quotes/10083, accessed February 2023

'And some of those are eating into our market share,' Herman bit back.

'Why should we change when all they do is copy us?' Freddie countered.

'I'm not suggesting FSS changes everything it does,' I interject. 'Your core product has been incredibly successful for almost fifteen years, but this does not mean it can and will survive. Deming explicitly warns us that...' I turned to the flipchart and wrote: 'Improvement is necessary for survival.'

'Survival is not guaranteed,' Herman observed, his face gloomy.

'Exactly,' I confirmed. 'The statistics show that between 1955 to 2014, 88% of the then Fortune 500 companies disappeared or dropped out of that ranking. The problem was, nobody at the time expected it.'[4]

Sabine furrowed her brow; this information obviously disturbed her. 'What went wrong back then?' she asked.

'That's a good question,' I turned to her, adding, 'you could say it was complacency on their part, that they felt entitled to longevity and didn't need to earn it.'

'Where does that mindset come from, though?' Sabine pressed further.

'From a misplaced reliance on an industrial legacy that began at the turn of the last century when the average lifetime of a company was expected to span

---

4   E Fry, *Fortune Magazine* (June 2, 2014), https://fortune.
    com/2014/06/02/first-fortune-500, accessed November 2022

eighty to a hundred years. Today, the forecast for new start-ups is totally different. Any guesses?'

'Twenty-five years,' Christoph suggested.

'Fifty?' Leon guessed.

I waited a moment for any other thoughts, but none was forthcoming. 'Ten years,' I said. 'The average lifetime of a company that starts today is ten years.'

Herman was visibly shocked, but Freddie let out a hearty laugh. They all looked at him, confused by his amusement. He stood up, clearly wanting to command the room as he leaned forward over the table. 'Then, my friends, we have nothing to worry about. Already FSS has bucked the trend. We have survived Luis' death cult. We won and you,' he jabbed his index finger toward me, 'just lost your own argument.' Turning to Herman, in a pleading tone, he said, 'Herman, please, do we really have to listen to any more of this crap? I think I can speak for us all in saying we've had enough of Luis' BS. This is wasting time. We've got a business to run. We've tried this Agile nonsense you seem so keen on, and did it work? Did we turn out software any faster? No. It's a waste of time, I'm telling you.' He stood waiting for Herman to finally agree with him. The air in the room felt heavy in the silence that followed.

I often observe similar early interventionist objections to my teachings and insights when a company is struggling, and I've learned not to take it personally. I understand where it comes from: people are scared by what they're learning; scared by the state of their business. They're also scared of change. For some, the best line of defence – especially when they feel personally threatened and in fear of exposure (which is almost always in their heads, magnified by their refusal to engage with change) – is to either stick their head in the sand, or to lash out noisily to guarantee they'll be heard. They assume that being heard means they will be listened to. Freddie wasn't having a go at me or my business philosophy, he was having a go at Herman. He'd inadvertently challenged Herman's authority and critical judgement in bringing me in to run this workshop. A workshop that is, I concede, provocative at times, but necessarily so – it is designed to force everyone's head out of the sand so that they can assess the landscape around them.

We were all waiting for Herman to respond to Freddie's outburst. He glanced toward me and I gave him a small, reassuring nod to let him know I was unthreatened, but it was clear that Herman was not OK. He leaned forward, clasping his hands in front of him in a tight knot, his knuckles white. He looked directly at Freddie and, in a measured tone, said:

'If you truly believe, Freddie, that what's happening here today is "a waste of time" then yes, I'd agree.'

Freddie snorted in triumph and swung back in his chair like a medieval king having just gorged on his supper. But his satisfaction would be short-lived. Herman continued, barely able to control his rising anger:

'*You* are the one wasting our time.'

Freddie looked astonished, for the first time his face flushed not from anger. Herman continued, 'It was my call to invite Luis here, my judgement, my intuition. I know in my heart that FSS is on borrowed time. Yes, we've outlived expectations, but that doesn't give any of us in this room the right to think we'll still be sitting here five, ten years from now. Far from it. Our old ways of operating won't see us through to our old age – and I, for one, haven't spent the best part of my entrepreneurial life in pursuit of failure. I think that we got it wrong with Agile in the past, that we viewed it simply as a way of working. Luis is trying to show us that Agile is not just a philosophy, it's a pragmatic necessity if we want to survive in these crazy times and beat the competition. Doing OK is not enough. We *must* change if we're to thrive. This is not a waste of my time, Freddie.'

'I agree,' Christoph said, 'even though I'm not sure yet *how* we'll change, I think we must at least be open to it.'

At this point, Freddie got up and walked out of the room, without saying a word.

'He'll be back. Once he calms down,' Herman said. I wasn't sure when that would be, but felt it was a positive step forward since it immediately lowered the temperature in the room. I also hoped it would give Freddie some time for cool-headed reflection. My presence was obviously rubbing him up the wrong way and his position was fixed before I had even begun. In many ways, I sympathise with the Freddies of the world. Many have worked their whole lives, set in their ways of organising business silos, operating on principles that have been drummed into them first at school then at college, which inevitably makes it hard for them to understand the real meaning of agility. When things seem to be going well, the concept of change, when it's not clear what needs to change and how, is an alien proposition. I sympathised with Freddie because he is a product of the conformist mindset of an education system that has shaped his practice toward delivering projects, whereas Agile is a mindset by which to organise a company's entire philosophy, not just software development.

'There was one thing Freddie said that I do kind of agree with,' Leon said.

'Please, I'd like to know,' I smiled back.

'We have tried implementing Agile, true, but I wouldn't say it helped us release software any faster than if we hadn't.' This was an excellent observation, and I was pleased Leon had raised it.

'It's a common misconception that Agile will deliver software faster,' I explained. 'That could not be further from the truth. With Waterfall, it takes twelve months; with Agile, it's exactly the same. The speed of delivery is the same because the amount of work is the same.'

'What's the advantage of Agile over Waterfall then?' Leon asked again. 'I'm guessing there is one, but if the speed of delivery doesn't change then I'm not yet clear on what that is.'

'Me neither, if I'm honest,' Sabine added.

'The big difference,' I said, 'is that with Waterfall you and your customers will only see the result at the end of the twelve months, but what's delivered may not be fully ready and only after twelve months of development do you get that feedback. Agile, on the other hand, delivers faster feedback because it allows you to rapidly deliver small pieces of your bigger puzzle and collect immediate feedback that can then be integrated into the software product. Agile is more of a continuation.'

'But is there a plan? It sounds like you develop it, test it, rejig it and then start all over again. Isn't that a little haphazard?' Leon asked, intelligently. It was another good question.

'A lot of people believe that Agile is just constantly adapting without a bigger plan. In reality, Agile has a more detailed plan than Waterfall.' I turned over the sheet on the flipchart and began to write up the seven layers of alignment as I spoke.

Seven Layers of Alignment

I opened the floor to questions and observations.

'We've not seen Agile expressed in this way,' Jonas said, 'I don't recall any sort of plan before. This seems much more documented than I was led to believe.

In fact, I was led to believe that documentation isn't Agile.'

'Not true,' I said, 'but again it's a common mistake to think that you don't need any documentation because you're implementing Agile. Agile still requires documentation for legal reasons – for ways of working, for knowledge sharing, for thousands of different reasons.'

'Are you saying that Agile alone will fix all our problems?' Christoph asked. 'Because we've got a lot to fix by all accounts.'

'Again, that's not true,' I reply. 'In all probability, when you first begin to implement Agile you'll discover even more problems.' I could sense their alarm and dismay, so quickly added, 'Agile creates transparency across your entire organisation and shines a light on problem areas that have remained hidden for years.'

'Such as?' Herman asked.

'For example, how your organisation is dysfunctional, operating via a myriad of independently run silos that impede the flow of communication between them, which in turn prevents total alignment across the business.'

'I see,' Herman nodded, 'so instead of *fixing* our problems, it will highlight them all, especially the ones we choose not to see or acknowledge.'

'If we adopt Agile in the way you suggest,' Christoph mused, 'does that mean not committing to release dates? At least with Waterfall we know that the deadline will always be twelve months ahead.

That's typically how we've released new software products to the market.'

'Does it always work?' I was curious to know.

'Well, admittedly we don't always get it right at the end of that period, so we have to make adjustments based on what our customers tell us, but…' Christoph tailed off as the penny dropped.

'With Agile, you might have ironed those issues out sooner by releasing incrementally, and still met your twelve-month deadline,' I suggested.

Christoph smiled. I continued, 'With Agile, you still commit to dates, but the emphasis is different. With Waterfall, you run the risk of postponement by trying to achieve success with fixed requirements and scope. In that scenario, the schedule becomes a problem when things don't go as expected. This has an impact on the dates and the quality. With Agile, it's completely different. You fix the date and then the scope changes. I'm not suggesting that Agile is better or worse than Waterfall. That's another huge misconception. It all depends on what you want to achieve. Agile works well in unpredictable, complex environments, such as software development.'

'Does that mean that in more predictable environments, such as building a house, Waterfall delivers because in general the requirements don't change?' Christoph asked.

'Exactly,' I said, adding, 'with Agile, the product backlog with the OKRs, together with the strategic vision of the company, are all aligned. All the pieces of the puzzle fit together.'

'Ah, I think I'm beginning to get it,' Christoph beamed.

'My impression had been that Agile requires a lot less discipline, totally different to what you're saying,' Jonas remarked, having been quietly pondering for most of the session.

'There is a reason for everything that's done in Agile; each part connects to the bigger strategy. Agile is the umbrella for different methodologies with their own rules and principles – Scrum, for example. Agile, whatever shape or form it comes in, won't function unless it's disciplined. It's not just a project management approach to running a business.'

'Okay,' Jonas said, looking puzzled again, 'it might create more flexibility, but doesn't that lead to less stability as a result, if we're constantly reacting to feedback on products that aren't yet at their peak?'

I had been expecting this question at some point and I was pleased that Jonas was trying to tie up the loose ends in his head. I replied carefully.

'The principle on which Agile relies is that everything you build is a small piece of the intended final outcome, but it's still 100% fit for purpose. That means each iteration is finished to a high standard; it's tested and ready to go to production. It's completely stable.'

At this point, I pull up illustrations based on the ideas of Jeff Patton that neatly visualise the key differences between Agile and Waterfall.[5]

---

5   J Patton, 'Don't know what I want, but I know how to get it' (Jeff Patton & Associates, 2008), www.jpattonassociates.com/dont_know_what_i_want, accessed February 2023

Incrementing Towards a Fully Formed Idea – Waterfall

Iterating Ideas – Agile

I explain that the Waterfall mindset calls for a fully formed idea upfront, but the whole picture isn't revealed until the project is completed. By contrast, Agile is more interactive and allows developers to progress an early idea all the way through to realisation, making course corrections as they go based on feedback. Crucially, this also allows them to stop if they encounter diminishing returns. In an iterative process, you build a rough version of an idea, validate it, then slowly build up the quality.

Herman and his colleagues took in the images, which clearly showed that, while Waterfall requires developers to have a full-detail vision of where they want to end up, Agile expects that their vision will shift.

I explain the implications in more detail. 'In terms of applying this to software design, similar to what you do at FSS, Waterfall is a phased approach that begins with a period of analysis followed by design, then coding and, finally, testing.'

'That sounds familiar,' Leon interjected, and there were murmurs of agreement from everyone else.

'Which explains,' I continued, 'why the actual product, or project, is only ever achieved at the end of the cycle, when it may be discovered that it doesn't suit the customers.'

'Yes, that definitely sounds familiar,' Leon confirmed, the pain of recognition clear in his fading smile. I moved on swiftly, 'Agile software development breaks everything into smaller pieces, managed by a dedicated SWAT team.'

'You mean, a team to do analysis, discuss the design, build and test?' Jonas asked.

Herman jumped in to answer before I could: 'The big issue with Waterfall is that while we do get a lot achieved over the whole development phase, we're taking a big risk because nothing is usable – and so not generating any revenue – until we get to the end of the process.'

'Whereas with Agile,' Sabine chimed in, 'by developing iteratively in small pieces, we could actually release 5% of the total, then build up to 10% and so on, but each piece is usable in itself and can be monetised.'

'That's exactly it,' I said, 'so you can sell as you go. It may not be a perfect solution, but it's a usable one.'

'Agile actually accelerates value delivery, doesn't it?' Herman observed.

'Now I see,' Leon piped up, 'it's not about Agile delivering faster; the delivery time is the same as with Waterfall, but with Agile we can accelerate the value delivery because we can deliver small pieces to the market as we go.'

'And respond to feedback,' Sabine added.

'Do we still make money?' Herman asked.

'That's your call,' I said. 'But you can sometimes charge a low price for the small pieces you release. Not the full price, but enough to deliver value to your company as well as the customer. Using Waterfall, on the other hand, runs the risk of not delivering any revenue at all at the end of twelve months if the product isn't fit for market. Worse still, the market value of a feature decreases over time.'

'Meaning?' Herman asked.

I explained, 'If you release a product to the market one year with certain specs, only to release another product with the same specs a year later, you can't charge the same price because it's now outdated. Also, as soon as your competitors begin to release the same or compatible features, it becomes a commodity and your product's value decreases. The trick to making more money faster is to release new features when they're your USP, not a commodity.'

At this point, Christoph became animated again. 'Let me get this straight,' he said, 'because traditionally we've always been concerned about ROI. Each time we release a new product or feature, we always measure that against risk failure which, let's be honest, has been a regular occurrence around here recently. Which perhaps explains Freddie's attitude today. Nevertheless, if I'm getting this right, Luis, my understanding is that with Agile, we could potentially manage our risk more effectively through iterative development and incremental testing in the market-place with feedback from the customer.'

'Precisely,' I concur, 'and so with Agile the risks get smaller and smaller with each iteration and validation. Risk is much less of a worry for the whole team over the development period. With Waterfall, the risk – and the pressure on your people – remains high until the product is validated. Or it isn't.'

'I like the idea of avoiding the death march and burnout,' Jonas said, semi-joking. 'How many times have we been right up against the deadline for proving a product hypothesis, with pressure mounting up, then we have to wait until launch to see if it pays off. Nobody knows how it's going to be received or whether it's going to deliver any revenue. It sucks.'

Jonas' words hit home and everyone in the room seemed to feel the power of what he'd just said. They'd all been there before, but it was beginning to dawn on them that Agile was more than simply a way of working, as they'd been led to believe. They were beginning to realise that with Waterfall, they were guessing what the customer wanted based on their past success, when in the fast-paced, highly competitive digital age, customer expectations had changed completely.

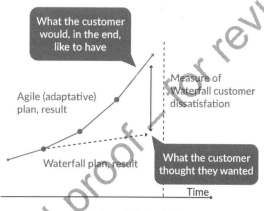

Agile vs Waterfall

One of the major benefits of Agile is that it allows a business to adapt, sprint by sprint, to meet customer expectations and, crucially, to quickly change direction to keep the customer happy. It's not simply a matter of delivering an end product outlined in a contract, after a long development period, especially if it then fails to deliver.

I expand further on the additional benefits of Agile, explaining to the group that, 'since it's a transparent process, it involves the customer at every iterative turn and you're always able to deliver the most important and valuable work. The moment you hit a problem area, it's clear where it sits within the process.

It's not a nasty surprise at the end of twelve months that can easily sour supplier–client relations. Instead, you'll be able to explain the bump in the road and work together to ensure you can always present the most valuable, working product to them, on budget and on time.'

This was the perfect opportunity for a ten-minute break to allow the group to process the bones of Agile as a business philosophy, the explanation of which had challenged their initial expectations. After the break, I would be putting them to the test.

The Agile vs Waterfall exercise

With still no sign of Freddie, the group returned to the conference room. This was a shame, because I'd hoped he would be more open to what they were about to learn. In this practical part of the workshop, I asked them to draw up a cumulative cash flow graph for two scenarios:

- Scenario A: A product in a Waterfall way that takes twelve months to come to market. Assume you have a team of five people and each is paid $5k per month salary. After twelve months, you release the product, which starts to generate $100k per month.

- Scenario B: The same product, this time developed using Agile, with the same team and salaries. In this scenario, every quarter you can release a piece of the product that generates $25k extra in revenue per month.

When these two scenarios are compared side by side, the differences are stark. In Scenario A (Waterfall), the breakeven point is reached after fifteen months.

Breakeven Point in Waterfall

In Scenario B (Agile), the breakeven point is reached after just eight months.

'You're kidding me. A full seven months earlier?' Herman said, his eyes glued to the charts.

'Yes. Incredible, isn't it?' I replied. 'You can see how Agile accelerates value delivery and improves cashflow. That's not just useful for start-ups, but for pretty much any business of a similar size to FSS.'

'Indeed,' he said, incredulous, 'just look at the difference in the money on the Waterfall side, it takes so much more upfront – $300k as opposed to $75k in Agile.'

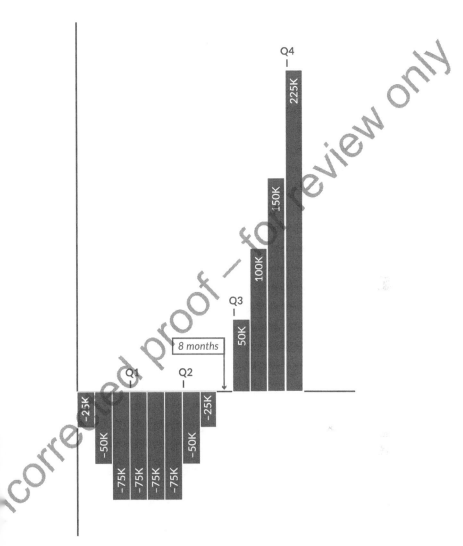

Breakeven Point in Agile

'Because you're able to release small pieces of the product to the market sooner and generate income that then gets ploughed back into the ongoing development costs. There's no need to find the whole sum up front when it can be realised cumulatively.' I added, 'This is when Agile really comes into its own. You're all familiar with Scrum? That's where you start.'

'We've used Scrum before, but I've never seen anything like the results here,' Leon commented. 'Where did we go wrong?'

'It's a simple, but complex answer,' I said, at which they all laugh. 'I doubt that when you last used Agile it was as connected to the overall strategy as I recommend it should be. Often, it's a quick fix, a one-off exercise that is unlikely to deliver without the executive leadership team's complete commitment and buy-in.'

Their laughter quickly drained away as they recognised this to be true, but they were fully engaged as I continued: 'Following Scrum, we identify the highest priority product backlog before launching into a two-week (ten business days) sprint. We're drawing on pretty much the same departments as you would in Waterfall, so no real surprises – product management, architecture development, testing and quality assurance. Except in Waterfall, they'd all be working independently in their own silos, occasionally butting heads with another, disagreeing here, holding things up there. Starting with Scrum, you bring all this expertise together in one cross-functional team.'

'And who heads up this team? What does it look like?' Herman asked, ready to take notes.

'The Scrum team usually has between five and nine people who completely self-manage,' I told him.

'No team leader?' Herman asked baffled.

'Correct,' I confirmed. 'There are no managers or team leaders because you need to avoid hierarchy in the team to enable self-management. There will be a Scrum master for every team – each Scrum master can handle at least two teams – and the product owner is fully dedicated to the team.'

'Who's the product owner?' Leon asked. 'Could that be one of the exec team?'

'No,' I corrected him, 'any one of you may end up as the head of the product start-up team focusing on the strategic vision, looking ahead to the next two to five years.'

'Like a CEO for the product?' Herman asked.

'Yes,' I agreed, 'whereas the product owner is responsible for its immediate practical implementation over the three to six months of the cycle.'

'In which case, they're the lynchpin,' Leon jumped back in, 'they ensure that the team keeps on track with the agreed vision, drives business value, walks in the shoes of the customer and liaises with management to plan releases.'

'Whereas the Scrum master runs the team meetings, enforces the job behaviour, removes impediments, attends to integration and protects the team from outside influence. Is that the idea?' Jonas added. I was sensing a revelation.

'That's it,' I confirm, 'this is the first step to understanding the true nature of Agility. But theory is never enough – agility is just a word unless it works in complete tandem with continuous delivery.'

It had been an intense hour or so and not without drama, thanks to Freddie's exit. That wasn't my problem – I'm never in a boardroom to get involved in the internal power politics of a business (although often, I'm called in when politics has brought a business to its knees). All that aside, the time, effort and concentration of Herman and his colleagues was beginning to pay off. I could sense there had been a significant mindset shift for each of them in individual ways, but also collectively. I could also see that this shift was most noticeable in their awareness of what Agile represented versus Waterfall. Prior to this session, they'd considered Agile to be chaotic, undisciplined and unplanned, but they'd re-evaluated that perception. Were they to carry on as they had been, they may be heading toward a much more chaotic future – releasing more products while needing to tailor hundreds of others to suit individual customer needs.

Most notably, though, there seemed to be a realisation of just how stuck in their silo mentality they'd become, which had led to increasing dysfunctionality and disagreement. Their current trajectory was already suggesting no sustainable long-term growth – in fact, quite the opposite. Herman had worked long and hard to carve out FSS's niche in the market, but, like many businesses that have failed to keep pace, their once dominant market position was under threat. Everyone around the table was beginning to reassess.

The risk the business faced now was dropping off the edge of the business landscape within only a matter of years – just like the titans of the twentieth century had disappeared from the ranks of the Fortune 500.

THE ADAPT METHODOLOGY™
PROJECT TO PRODUCT SCORECARD

Three sessions completed. Evaluate whether you are leading an outdated project-centric business or a modern product-led company at: https://bit.ly/ Scorecard_ProductFirst_Book

4

Continuous Delivery

A s we resumed, I was relieved to see that Freddie had re-joined the group. I'd noticed that during the break he and Herman had been locked into what looked to be an animated conversation behind the closed doors of a glass-walled office. Whatever had been aired in private, there was a dignified silence when they both emerged. I wasn't sure which way this would go, but Freddie brushed past me into the board-room and took his seat without acknowledging the others as they returned. He sat there for a few moments fiddling with his smartphone while I set up the laptop for the session that was about to start. Herman was the last to take his seat and it was obvious that the two men had exchanged some frank words. I was anxious – I don't like tension in my teaching space, as it can be disruptive and unproductive. But before I could begin, Freddie coughed loudly to gain everyone's attention.

'I just wanted to say,' he began, hesitating a little, 'that I realise my actions earlier were not what's expected of me and so, Luis, Herman, everyone, I would like to apologise.'

There was an immediate, palpable sense of relief all round.

'Thank you. It's OK,' I told him, just happy that I would be able to return to the session and put this behind us.

'No, it's not OK,' Freddie went on, 'but you have to understand my position. I've been at this company from the moment it opened its doors for business and I only ever have its best interests at heart. I'll be the first to admit that lately we're not doing as well as we could and that we should all pull together in our efforts to find solutions. Whether I agree or not with what's being said in these workshops is a matter of personal opinion, but I'm willing to listen to all the options.'

'Freddie, we're all on the same page here,' Leon reassured him.

'I know. I shouldn't have let my feelings run away with me like I did, but it's because I care about this business. I'm prepared to accept that what Luis is telling us may be useful in determining how we see through our plans to expand. If I'm not part of that conversation, then I don't deserve my place at this table. That's all I have to say.'

As I've mentioned, I've come across more than one Freddie in my time and invariably they're in IT. They have the keys to the digital front door of the business and nobody likes to feel they're being locked out of their own house. Usually, that perception is born from some level of fear. Nobody at FSS intended to lock Freddie out. Without the support of IT in driving it, the necessary change would be impossible.

When a change like misguided or ill thought-through Agility initiatives is introduced, rejected and then reintroduced, I can understand someone like Freddie's frustrations and concern that their role was under threat. IT department personnel are often the target of others' anger when things go wrong. The difference in what I do, is I bring all parties together on a level playing field. Consensus and collaboration going forward is key to successful Agile implementation – not finger pointing and blame.

I smiled at Freddie to let him know that I was OK, no further discussion was needed, and we were ready to begin.

'Earlier, I touched upon the concept of continuous delivery. What do I mean by that?'

'Pushing more and more product to the market,' Leon suggested.

'Test, test, test,' Jonas added.

'Yes. But there's a right and a wrong way to do that,' I said.

'Based on…?' Herman asked.

'Based on how testing is carried out in the traditional manner and how it is adapted for the digital marketplace,' I clarified.

The team exchanged looks. Freddie leaned on the table, stroking his chin. I had their full attention.

'One way to visualise continuous delivery is to imagine a factory assembly line, where cross-functional engineers work on various parts of the software as it moves through its lifecycle. Traditionally, teams might only deliver software every few months and, because of the manual process, it's prone to error.'

'Hold on a minute,' Jonas interrupted me, 'if we're talking software, how can it be manual?'

'The key is in the word "traditional". What do you think that refers to, even for a business like FSS, producing software solutions?'

'Ah,' Herman said, understanding sinking in, 'you mean structurally?'

'Exactly. Which often means that pieces of the delivery package go back and forth between teams that are separated by silos. It's a long, drawn out and expensive exercise where the final package is assembled at the eleventh hour after varying degrees of in-fighting, politics and hold-ups, and even then, the product might not work properly. Everyone feels deflated, angry, dispirited and teams vow to never repeat it again.'

'Sounds familiar,' Freddie remarked.

'But with continuous delivery, that software can be delivered to whichever schedule you choose, be that several times a day, once a week – as often as you want. The difference compared to traditional delivery methods is, it's always in a releasable state. This has two distinct advantages, which are....?' I tailed off, inviting the group to give their thoughts.

'We're releasing software all the time; it's not a one-off effort,' Leon said.

'We operate as cross-functional teams and not in silos,' Christoph added.

'I'm guessing,' Jonas joined in, 'that those teams are made up of developers, testers, database analysts and operations?'

'All contributing to a single path to production,' Leon repeated.

'Good. Does that sound like what you currently do?' I asked.

The group agreed that it didn't.

'That means,' I continued, 'we're not just talking about developer changes here; it also relies on changes to the infrastructure.'

'So the aim is that a single team builds the entire package and tests it, is that right?' Herman asked.

'Yes,' I confirmed, 'and once it's passed all those checks, it's potentially ready to be released to users. When a problem is discovered, the users will inevitably offer feedback quickly, which tells the team members what they need to fix. The product is continually updated until all the acceptance criteria are met, when it progresses to production.'

'Let me check if I understand this,' Freddie said, and all heads turned toward him. 'Continuous delivery involves all parts of software development, where all team members work on a single path to production so that it reaches users more quickly.'

'In a more predictable manner, yes. Let me show you,' I said, writing the sequence on the flipchart:

1. Build package

2. Unit testing

3. Integration testing

4. Acceptance testing

5. Ship it

6. Users provide feedback based on their usage

'From this, you can see that you begin with the least expensive, basic tasks,' I explained.

'At API level?' Jonas asked.

'Yes,' I said, 'and then move onto the ones that are the most difficult, regarding the user interface.'

'They're the most demanding, in terms of time,' Jonas added.

'Which is why I say, leave them to the end,' I said.

Leon interjected: 'I think I know where this is heading, but if I'm right, then most of our backlog and expenditure problems are of our own making.' He exchanged a worried look with Jonas, who nodded silently to confirm he was thinking the same thing.

'What you're implying,' Freddie mused, 'is that it doesn't make any sense to start testing user interface until basic functionality is proven.'

'Exactly right,' I confirmed. 'If you think about testing a simple calculator, you'd want to check that two plus two equals four, as a basic test. The more time-consuming tests would be of its rendering – for example, are the digits shown correctly on the UI? It would be pointless to test the digital display rendering when the basic sum operation was faulty. Let's take this a stage further.'

'I thought you said this was simple?' Christoph quipped.

'It is, and automation is the key. What if that first stage of basic testing was automated, where the process of testing itself had been validated? The impact of having the basic functionalities tested is that fewer testers – by which I mean real people – are needed. They only carry out the UI part of the testing process, instead of the whole thing,' I explained.

'Making us more productive and efficient in the process,' Freddie remarked, impressed, adding, 'We really screwed up Agile, Herman. I told you.'

'We certainly did,' Herman smiled back at him, 'but even you didn't know why.'

'We all have our blind spots,' Freddie countered.

I continued, 'To be clear, once the testers have completed pre-production and all steps have been validated, the software can then be released automatically so that there's no need for further human involvement at all. When you reach that point, you know your organisation is operating with a high level of trust in its people and processes. In the banking sector, that's not possible because they're legally obliged to ensure that a human checks everything before anything goes live, but for businesses such as yours, you can enjoy full production line automation – should that be what you're aiming for.'

'Wow,' Sabine explained, 'that could free up so much time and resources that we could deploy elsewhere.'

'You mean for your marketing budget?' Freddie sniped.

'Why not?' Sabine snapped back.

'Continuous delivery would be the cherry on top, whichever way you look at it,' Herman observed, diffusing the tension before it escalated.

'It's about mindset,' I intervene, 'because in traditional organisations, software developers aren't always interested in the testing process. They're more focused on writing code because that's their silo. In more competent Agile organisations, software developers want to test their codes so that the business can achieve a fully automated pipeline because, as a result, they'll be able to run thousands of tests in a matter of minutes. That's not something you can do using humans. Let me show you what I mean.'

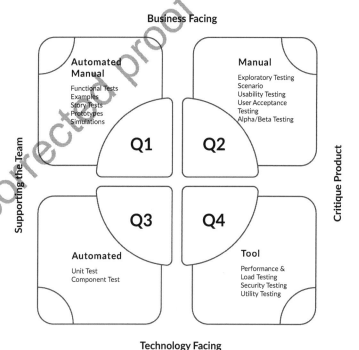

Testing Quadrants

I presented the above diagram, which visualises in a quadrant the differences between traditional manual and automated testing processes:

- Quadrants 1 and 2 are automated.

- Quadrant 3 is manual.

- Quadrant 4 is automated.

'Our testing quadrant would look quite different,' Freddie observed.

'In what way?' I asked.

'Well, we do get to the automated stage, but in the other three we've got manual, manual, manual built into our process. I don't think it's occurred to us that we could run automatic tests that are critical of the product without the need for human interaction. That seems to be the key difference between your approach and ours.'

'This new model shows us where we can be more productive and cost efficient, as Sabine said,' Herman added.

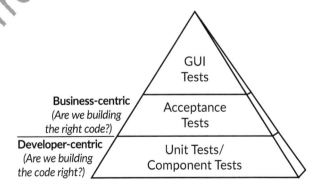

Test Automation Pyramid

I show them the diagram above, the Test Automation Pyramid, and ask, 'At the base of the pyramid, those unit/component tests are the most important. Why?'

'They're the ones that the developers can write, and that can be super automated,' Freddie answered.

'I don't understand. Why?' Christoph asked.

'Because when we change the code somewhere else in the product, those unit tests – assuming everything checks out – won't break the code. That means, where problems occur, if a code breaks somewhere down the chain, the automation arising from the unit tests will alert us to that. It doesn't have to be a person,' Freddie explained.

'Right, I get it,' Christoph said. 'In effect, user acceptance coding is a safety net that protects the developers if they change the coding, even though everything else is automated.'

'Which means these unit tests are developer-centric because *they* write the code, to ensure everything is well written and not broken,' Freddie re-emphasised.

'It's a process that continually interrogates,' Leon added.

'In which case, automation eliminates the need for whole groups of testers to be manually involved. Why? Because it knows whether it's building the right product, almost at warp speed compared to how we do things around here right now,' Freddie said triumphantly.

'It knows that 2 + 2 = 4,' Jonas said.

'And from a marketing perspective,' Sabine added, 'my team can brief our developers in a more refined fashion.'

'How do you mean?' Christoph asked.

'The tests can be based on the known behaviours the data has already identified. We're no longer working in the dark. In the future, we'll know what triggers customers to click through to content or a sales opportunity because we have intel on how they navigate the site.'

'In that case, we need more developers and fewer testers, because the automated testing code has in-built, already tested user acceptance,' Christoph said, answering his own question.

'That's how I see it,' Freddie concluded.

'Agreed,' Herman said.

With that, I wrapped up the session. Even as they were packing up to leave the room, they were already scheduling meetings in order to plan and strategise going forward.

Day One reflection

It had been a long day. These first three parts of the workshop are usually the most challenging for participants, not only because they have to take time out of their typically hectic schedules, but I'm also asking them to collectively buy into my methodology. In FSS, that was important since it highlighted how their normal practice was to operate across individual departmental lines. They had begun the workshop believing they were a digital business, but that was only partly true. Their customer offering may have been digital products, but they were developed, managed and serviced via non-digital pathways. Freddie's initial rejection of the ADAPT Methodology™ was rooted in his hostility toward Agile, which had been forced upon him and his team essentially because it felt 'digital'. It was not an exercise that had been broadened out to the rest of the business. What I was introducing was the idea that the silo mentality in their operations put up barriers to growth in the digital marketplace. As a business, they were failing to address their customers' pain. In fact, it was clear that FSS had lost sight of who its target customer was and what those pains might be. They needed to address this if they were to grow and scale as planned.

By the end of Day One, the team at FSS had begun to appreciate that my role was to help them realise they needed to progress beyond a standing still recovery, into discovery and onto continuous delivery.

THE ADAPT METHODOLOGY™ PROJECT TO PRODUCT SCORECARD

Four sessions completed. Evaluate whether you are leading an outdated project-centric business or a modern product-led company at: https://bit.ly/Scorecard_ProductFirst_Book

5
Product

I always approach the second day with a sense of optimism and enthusiasm. That's partly due to the fact that, during the previous ones, I've laid down the groundwork in building relationships with the people in the room, most of whom I would have never have met before and who, in all honesty, would probably have preferred not to have taken time away from their already busy schedules.

At FSS, by mid-morning on Day One, the discussions had grown energetic, forthright and tinged with a growing sense of curiosity in response to the challenges I was setting them. By the end of the first day, we all had the measure of each other and it was clear which pillars participants were eager to learn more about and which were still proving to be a barrier.

In that sense, the group represented a snapshot of the business, as the human face of its inner workings.

At the heart of everything I do is always the people. By the time we reconvene for the next sessions, we're all familiar with each other, but, more interestingly, as a leadership team they have uncovered their internal mechanisms and how they interact with each other. Because of the high-level nature of the discussions they had the day before, I could sense some relief that old grievances as well as the new challenges had been acknowledged within the safety of the boardroom. They'd discovered how to talk openly with each other about ideas that, when implemented strategically, would transform their business. The purpose was to look back only with a view to improving the future. They come to Day Two, therefore, revitalised in the knowledge that more challenges lay ahead but in a context of aspiration and ambition – which they would need, since the first topic of the day was product.

Day Two

'We know what our product is,' Freddie said immediately upon seeing the heading I've written on the flipchart, looking to the team for confirmation.

'Of course: software development,' Sabine confirmed, followed by a mock sigh, 'although I think we're about to be told otherwise?' She looked at me with a wry smile and the others laughed.

'That's what I'm worried about,' Freddie said. It wasn't clear whether he was joking.

'No, look,' Herman said emphatically, 'we're clear about what we do.'

'Tell me,' I encouraged him.

'It's simple. We create financial software solutions for our clients. The problem we have is figuring out where we're heading and how we scale in the digital marketplace. Right?'

Everybody around the table nodded silently. By now they knew that I wouldn't agree with them entirely, but it wasn't yet my place to let the cat out of the bag. Self-discovery is much more impactful than a lecture. I probe the team further. 'Is that what your current business model is based on?'

'Of course,' Herman replied, 'it's where we started and we have no intention of diversifying. You're not recommending that, I presume?' he asked.

'OK, let me get this straight,' I continued, 'the business model as you understand it is based around a single product – financial software?'

'Yes...' Herman confirmed, hesitant.

'And it's the same product, or range of out-of-the-box products, that clients choose from, depending on what level of service they're prepared to buy into?'

'Yes,' Herman confirmed, looking confused.

'Ah...' Christoph mused. All heads turned toward him. His cheeks suddenly flushed and he ran a hand through his hair.

'Well?' Freddie prompted.

'It's not quite that simple, is it?' Christoph began. 'Yes, on one level that's exactly what we do but...' he paused, 'we don't exactly have a range of products like Luis has described.'

'Of course we do,' Freddie jumped in, 'clients choose from our portfolio what suits their needs best.'

'That's the point,' Christoph sighed. 'We have a great portfolio, but in all honesty, no two clients end up with the same product.'

'That's because we give them what they want,' Freddie barked again, sounding more irritated than when he arrived. 'I call that great customer service.'

'In which case,' I interrupt, 'is the business model about customising products, client by client, and if so, is that reflected in the company strategic vision? Or, is it...'

Herman cut in '...centred around creating a range of parameter-led products that we then tweak individually in order to close the sale?' This was met with silence, no one making eye contact. 'The answer, Luis, is that our business model is *not* predicated on that level of customisation.' Herman's shoulders dropped.

'Yes, but we're giving them what they want. Surely that's what matters?' Freddie cut back in.

'Except each customer's product is treated as if it were a project. Customisation doesn't allow you to scale,' I suggested, 'which is fine, but not if that's where you want this business to go.'

'What if we do want to scale?' Leon asked, 'Isn't that the whole point of our proposed growth strategy, to be able to implement customisation when necessary?'

'So far, customisation has proved problematic for you because you've allocated too much of your internal resources to serving customers. You can solve that if you outsource and work with partners that will handle the customisation for you, which then allows you to scale the product.'

'By freeing up our resources to focus on developing new product?' said Leon, understanding settling in.

'It's a big shift in your thinking that you urgently need to address going forward. Right now, you believe you have a product; in fact, you've created series of customised products that can't possibly scale because each has been tailored to a single client as its own project,' I explained.

'Requiring us to meet ever increasing demands to tweak functionality on an individual basis as opposed to incrementally developing better products,' Leon finished for me.

This knowledge that the business was in fact project- not product-led was evidently a revelation. It was clear that the level of customisation they had reached was a nightmare to maintain, with each project demanding different features and coding, as well as customer support. 'If you want to break into mass market delivery, it's not a sustainable business model,' I suggested, 'especially as the pool of bigger clients has already been targeted.'

'Where do we go from here then?' Leon asked, his tone defeated.

'You could move away from the current high level of customisation and return to your core product offering by developing an SaaS[6] that's available in the cloud, targeting smaller clients that don't require any customisation. Today, I'll show you how you

6   Software as a service

can rethink and reboot your current business model using the Business Model Canvas tool, created by my colleague, Alex,' I replied.

'What will that do?' Freddie asked.

'It will show that your product *is* your business model,' I explained.

'I don't get it,' he responded.

'What that means is, product is more than the thing the customer buys. Your product is your entire business. To think about your product, you have to think about your business model.'

The Business Model Canvas

I could see understanding dawning on them as I pulled up the next slide: the Business Model Canvas.[7]

This Business Model Canvas comprises nine key areas that pose some challenging questions:

1. Who are the key partners that can help distribute your product?

2. What are the key activities that the business develops?

3. What are your key resources?

4. What is your value proposition?

---

7   'The Business Model Canvas' (Strategyzer, no date), www.strategyzer. com/canvas/business-model-canvas, accessed February 2023

5. What is your customer relationship?

6. By what channels do you reach your customers?

7. What is your customer segment?

8. What are your revenue streams?

9. What is the cost structure?

I explained to the team that by rethinking their business model in terms of the product, it would be easier to identify a clear strategy going forward. As an example, I challenged them to consider the difference between the video rental company, Blockbuster and digital disruptor, Netflix. I asked them to tell me what they thought the central product offering was for each.

'Easy. Rental entertainment,' Christoph suggested, 'the difference being in how it's distributed.'

'Blockbuster became obsolete when on-demand streaming became a thing,' Sabine added, 'and nobody wanted to walk across town to rent a video when they could just call it up on a screen, anytime, anyplace.'

'What if I were to disagree?' I asked.

'But the product is the same, surely?' Sabine replied, 'it's just the distribution channel that's changed.' Everyone in the room nodded their agreement.

'That's true, but what about Netflix – what would you say their product is?' I probed further.

'Like Christoph said, video entertainment… Oh, hang on a minute…' Sabine trailed off, before adding, 'I get it. *Netflix* is the product that customers buy, not their content. They sell subscriptions to a portal, which gives the customer access to content. They have key partners, such as media companies, to provide original and licensed content.'

'And ISPs[8], I presume?' Herman added.

'Exactly,' I confirmed. 'And so Netflix's key resources are…?'

'Its streaming platform and storage,' Christoph said, adding, 'and I'm guessing its key activities include a hell of a lot of marketing?'

'Consider how well Netflix has been able to scale its subscription service, where the customer chooses what they want to view. Its product is still the portal itself.'

'Could we begin to offer something similar, even though we're in a completely different field?' Jonas asked, suddenly interested in cloud potential.

'I think so,' Herman replied, matching Jonas' enthusiasm. 'Our web platform could be the place where people upload their invoices and billing cycles. Our value proposition would be one-stop easy accounting.'

'And our customers will be small business owners, which could be in the thousands – instead of a clutch of big financial institutions each wanting a bespoke solution,' Sabine thought out loud.

'I'm liking this,' Freddie beamed – this was perhaps the first time I'd seen him genuinely absorbing ideas and appreciating their potential. Herman leaned over and gave him a pat on the shoulder.

---

8   Internet service providers

'Just to be clear,' Christoph asked, 'would our cost structure then revolve around managing sales and marketing and platform development?'

'That'll be for you to identify once you firm up your strategic vision, but yes, I would think that's broadly correct,' I confirmed.

'This could mean that the way we do business fundamentally changes,' Herman announced, 'and yet our core offering – our content, as it were – remains pretty much the same.'

'How you do that business will also be key to FSS's transformation, which you'll discover in the organisational mastery session in the next part of the workshop,' I told them.

'But from now on we should begin building new products through the OKR process?' Herman asked.

'Yes, but there's no need to ditch your current products,' I said. 'You have a business that's generating revenue, there'd be no point in starting from scratch. You'll need that revenue so that you can invest in rebooting the business model based around product.'

'In effect, the existing business sponsors that,' Herman confirmed.

'Good,' Freddie added. 'I'd worry if we killed off what we already have without a means of supporting the new venture financially.'

'In which case, we need a plan to run the two in parallel with a view to mapping out the OKRs as soon as possible. We keep running a legacy product while developing the future one,' Herman said, to the agreement of the whole room.

'It's just knowing where to begin – what do customers want from this new product?' Christoph mused.

'That's a good point,' I said, 'and when we arrive at the Transformation and Organisational Mastery pillar you'll see that innovation is central to product discovery. It's where you take prototypes to the market and run a series of tests. This normally occurs in parallel with software development at the end of an OKR or in preparation for the next.'

'This is great,' Sabine said, 'because we can measure and react to customer feedback more rapidly than if we spent months creating a product, then releasing it only to then have to go back and rework the whole offer. This way, we can release and modify while still earning from the product itself.'

'Just like Apple does with the iPhone,' Christoph ventured. 'That's innovation in action.'

'Correct,' I said, 'and the beauty of it is that even if you have a great idea but usability needs more work, you can use Google Sprint as the springboard during the innovation week of the Transformation pillar for product discovery and incorporate innovation into your product development.'

'It means changing our mindset, doesn't it?' Leon said.

'You mean about our process?' Freddie asked.

'We should be thinking of this as a lean start-up, not a series of projects,' Leon explained.

'Led by product managers,' added Sabine.

'Yes,' Leon agreed, 'and then whatever we create, the business model allows it to be repeatable and scalable.'

'That's true,' I confirmed, 'because sometimes the difference between success and failure is just a variable in the business model, not the product itself.'

'How so?' Freddie interjected, though I could sense he was interested in this line of thought. I told him, 'The product will still be the same, but if you choose the wrong channel, the wrong partner or the wrong marketing strategy, that's the fail. It's not the product's fault.'

'We go from focusing on project output to product outcome. It's a much more streamlined, productive approach,' Leon admitted.

'Bringing us back to the OKRs,' concluded Herman.

'Proving that Agile isn't the brains behind success,' I said before turning to Freddie: 'I completely get where your antagonism came from when I first mentioned Agile.' Freddie blushed and muttered something that sounded apologetic. 'Don't get me wrong,' I continued, 'Agile is a great way to facilitate development, but it doesn't know what the customer wants. All it guarantees is that you'll be able to produce something and produce it well. In fact, Agile can kill a business if it's not associated with the right product.'

'If you're producing crap, then all you're good at is producing crap quickly,' Freddie said, much to everyone's amusement, including me.

'But with a fully integrated product strategy in place, with Agile you can accelerate that delivery to market more confidently,' I said.

'Who wants to waste time producing beautiful software that serves no real purpose?' Leon quipped.

Herman was looking thoughtful. Speaking quietly he said, 'You know, Luis, we thought we *were* Agile.'

Freddie rolled his eyes. 'It was a tick-box exercise. Agile – it's the buzzword, everyone else is doing it, so we should, too. We didn't think it through. OK, I had no time for it – I admit it. For years we've been pushing out product that customers don't need or want. No wonder we haven't grown as much as we wanted, much less scaled up. We've been pissing into the wind.'

Harsh as it was, the room knew this to be true.

'Agreed,' Herman said sadly, 'It's clear to me now that our current product strategy is completely wrong.'

'On the bright side,' Leon said, 'when we do have our products well defined and strategised, Agile will make them fly.'

'If you work though the Business Model Canvas mechanism, you'll see that the world of discovery leads to faster delivery, linked by Agile,' I said, adding, 'Continuous product discovery is the gateway to any new feature or product line you want to develop. Any new target segment or target customer needs to involve some discovery. In fact...' I paused to take in the moment, all eyes were trained on me, 'it's also about strategy discovery and goals discovery. And that's what I want us to think about in the next session, about implementing a process that integrates cycles of discovery and delivery.'

'You mean, you're going to convert me into an Agile fan?' Freddie joked.

'Not only that,' I replied, 'you'll end up asking yourself where you'd be without it.'

The anticipation of what they might be on the brink of achieving was palpable in the room as we took a break.

The intention of this session was to link back to the first pillar, Approach, as a cornerstone of the overall business model. Having that early clarity in identifying the customer avatar and creating content through targeted engagement is key to creating the right product. The business model is then predicated on delivering that product, instead of undertaking projects, shifting focus from outputs to outcomes, based on:

- Market need

- Knowing their customers

- Identifying the value proposition

- Developing the market strategy

I could see Sabine thinking hard, quickly typing notes into her iPad, before she summarised her thoughts out loud:

'Using "Approach" as a key channel within the Business Model Canvas shifts the strategic focus away from outputs to outcomes. It makes sense of the idea that our product is our business model.'

'To add to that,' Christoph said, 'product is more than an object or service the customer buys.'

I agreed with both. When thinking about what your product is, it's essential to consider the whole business model, including all the channels for revenue, to identify:

- Key resources

- Value proposition

- Customer relationships and segments

- Cost structure

THE ADAPT METHODOLOGY™ PROJECT TO PRODUCT SCORECARD

Five sessions completed. Evaluate whether you are leading an outdated project-centric business or a modern product-led company at: https://bit.ly/Scorecard_ProductFirst_Book

6
Continuous Discovery

When I stepped back into the boardroom twenty minutes later, Freddie, Sabine and Leon were chatting in an animated huddle. Each was putting forward blue sky ideas from their own perspective following the introduction to the Product pillar. The thought of scaling the business into a market beyond customisation had fired up their imaginations, but what was interesting was that they weren't talking about reinventing the wheel, but recalibrating based on the Business Canvas Model. It was like turning on a tap full stream, as opposed to the drip-by-drip world they'd become accustomed to. It seemed that now they were intent on filling the bathtub as fast as they could. I didn't want to interrupt this flow of creative thinking because they'd naturally fallen into the embryonic, mini start-up mentality that underpins everything I advocate – bringing people with the right expertise into the product development team from different departments from the outset.

When they realised that we were ready to begin, they gave me their full attention. They had already made fantastic progress. What's more, the one person who had come to these workshops with an impediment mindset, had set himself free. I turned to Freddie and asked, 'How do you feel about Agile now?'

He opened his arms wide, 'I'm all ears.' I knew he would be more receptive now to what would follow in this continuous product discovery session – if I could convince him that he could be the brains behind it, he'd discover that it was his foot on the accelerator pedal. The speed at which they'd progress would be determined by him – and the whole team would be working as one.

'Everything has its own cycle,' I resumed, 'and continuous delivery depends entirely on discovery.'

'How long do we need to keep discovering for? Is there ever an end point?' Jonas asked.

'That's a great question,' I replied. 'Discovery means learning about something new, or previously unknown. That could be something hidden, or unexpected. If we relate that to continuous delivery, it could be expressed in a business context as "continuous discovery". For example, in Scrum, usually there are fixed cycles of the same length, but there's no guarantee that each cycle will result in discovery. Discovery isn't fixed in time. You may spend one day or one week in discovery cycles, dependent on the product and/or the industry. Ultimately, discovery means continuous learning. That's key to delivering business outcomes. It's the build–measure–learn correlation that applies to teams, or value streams, orchestrated by the product manager.'

'Does that mean we might be producing stuff that never gets used?' Leon asked, a serious look on his face.

'OK, let me be frank with you,' I replied, matching my tone to his expression. 'Agile doesn't reduce the waste of overproduction; anyone claiming that it does is misrepresenting it. The process does, however, inform the business's decision on what to build, but that decision is based on the knowledge and insights gained from discovery. Being fast and adaptable doesn't prove anything, but beginning that process as a lean start-up is key to continuous product discovery.'

'Which suggests,' Freddie interrupted, 'that in any initial product lifecycle, that's where we do most discovery. As that cycle matures, so does the product.'

'And over time, you do less discovery because you're building on that continuous learning process,' Sabine said.

'Precisely,' I agreed, 'but, more importantly, you also begin to deliver more. There's an additional benefit to be derived from this process…'

I paused, waiting for the room to respond, but they said nothing, so I continued: 'The product teams are no longer operating in silos, where one dreams up a concept and leaves it to another to deliver. What's needed are teams that do everything – which I saw the beginnings of when I walked back into this room.'

'It's not just discovery, then,' Herman pondered.

'No,' I continued, 'it's about bringing the minds of the entire business into a product team. Depending on the size of the business, sometimes the product manager that leads the digital growth team will also be the product owner, especially in scale-ups, but there will always be a need to differentiate the two main functions of discovery and delivery.'

'So who does what?' Christoph asks.

'Delivery can be left to the team. Discovery is a task that needs to be more in tune with the market and should be in alignment with the company strategy, so that can be led by the relevant product manager.'

The product manager is the person who 'owns,' and so is responsible for, the success of the product, from concept to market. This is the person who talks to customers and orchestrates engineering, design, marketing and sales. In today's lean environment, this person doesn't manage the people; they manage the product, the value and the process.

'The problem is, many companies still haven't evolved enough to do this well,' I told them.

'I think we can safely say that statement applies to us,' Herman mused.

'Which is why you reached out to me,' I said, 'but I think you now appreciate that, in order to survive and thrive, you need to evolve and adapt. FSS isn't alone – many businesses still operate in functional silos, which is a huge mistake in the digital marketing landscape.'

'What does the evolutionary journey look like?' Jonas asked.

'Obviously, at the start of any new product journey you'll run product discovery. In FSS, when you need to identify new features for your current products, you'll go through that same product discovery process, as well as the innovation process, which I will outline in the organisational mastery sessions.'

'What exactly are we supposed to be discovering?' Jonas asked.

I turned to the flipchart and wrote:

- The market opportunity

- The business model

- The size of the market

- The target segment and the customer needs

'Now, you can start discovering your MVP[9] and how that evolves into a market-fit product, learning how to incorporate any new functionalities and then how to scale. This is continuous discovery running in parallel with continuous delivery. It allows you to build fast and reliably, at the same time learning what it is you need to build.'

'That's a heavy responsibility for one product manager to shoulder,' Christoph suggested.

'I don't agree,' I replied, 'if you look at the skill set for a digital product manager, yes, it's a difficult role spanning a high number of areas. But some of those

---

9   Minimal viable product

skills are what we'd term "soft skills", the typical traits that characterise any leader.'

'Ah, you mean like negotiation, communication, influence and leading without authority?' Herman said.

'All those qualities, yes,' I agreed, 'but the product manager isn't actually managing anybody, which is probably one of the most difficult aspects of the role.'

'That's because they can't order any of us about,' Freddie smirked.

'True,' I say, 'but they are leading a product all the same. They're leading vision, a strategy with a view to creating success. They're orchestrating the entire discovery and delivery process and carrying a lot of people with them. That's not easy by any stretch of the imagination.'

'So much for being "soft",' Freddie quipped.

'And then there are the hard skills. Meaning, what do they need to know in order to perform the role? Where do they begin with discovery? What techniques and technology should they rely on to build the prototypes? Which ones work best in the different stages of the product lifecycle? Add to that defining the business model, building the product strategy and devising a plan to win in the marketplace – how will they beat their competitors? Who and what is the market? What does the industry look like?'

'Wow, that *is* a lot,' Christoph sighed.

'Yes. But remember, the core element of any digital product company is the product team, or even a team of teams, involved in cycles of discovery combined with cycles of delivery. These people do everything. There are no silos locked away in sales, or marketing, or engineering, or data or business intelligence – it's a team. This will be a huge change going forward. Companies exist to deliver products and services to the market. In which case, why do so many split themselves into silos or functions?'

'We should be organising based on products, shouldn't we?' Freddie observed. The entire room nodded in agreement.

Freddie continued, 'I think that's been part of my "problem" with Agile. I know more about it than I perhaps let on – at least I thought I did. Herman's always suggesting I need to go to these damn conferences, watch this webinar, read that book–'

'For your own good,' Herman interjected, laughing, 'and so that you could regale us with your newfound wisdom.'

'For all the good that did,' Freddie joined in the banter, but turned serious again. 'I've read so much material and content on Agility in the last fifteen years, I've gone numb to the extent that none of this "cultural change" thinking makes any sense. One person says Scrum is better than Kanban, another says the opposite. My point is, nobody's talking about product. Where is the product? In fact, who cares about the product? Nobody. Until you came along, Luis. Everyone leaves that responsibility to the business owners, the development managers, the traditional product managers or the project managers. What you're saying about product and continuous delivery is enlightening. I've come around to the idea that FSS needs to start taking care of product in the Agile space and learn what we need to know first in order to deliver good product to the market.'

There was a collective murmur of agreement around the room, interrupted by Herman who said, with conviction, 'It's clear, yes – we need to rethink and reset on so many levels.'

'I'm happy to hear that,' I said, 'because now I'd like you to do an exercise. I want you to create a business model for a hypothetical business based on the criteria we've just discussed.'

I outline a scenario in which I am approached by a friend who wants me to invest $50k into a cloud-based financial solutions service idea they want to develop into a business for Denmark. I ask the group, 'That's a huge amount of money to ask from an individual. Now knowing me and my thoughts on product, what do you think my first step would be?'

Leon shoots up his hand, 'Analyse the market opportunity – how big is it? Is it something the market needs?'

'Yes, so assuming I carry out some preliminary research and the results are favourable, I have another question forming…'

'If you invest, when will you get your money back?' Jonas suggested.

'And how much will you potentially earn?' Leon added.

'That's jumping ahead too fast,' I said, 'remember the cycle.'

After looking at her notes, Sabine spoke up: 'First, you look for the problem to solve and then design, or define, the solution. Then you want to know, is there a market for the product? If so, can you build it and create a repeatable, sustainable business model?'

'Yes,' I confirmed. 'So in the initial phase, there'll be a lot of continuous discovery and validation. What happens when I approach the product market fit?'

'You reduce the risk and presumably invest more,' said Freddie.

'After which you push the accelerator for revenue, but you're still not going to assign a huge team of developers to it,' Christoph said.

'Why not?' I asked him.

'Because you still don't know if people will buy it to any large degree.'

'There is something I can do, however, which is…?'

'You could create a tentative business model and, based on that, explore some options,' Leon said.

'Great. We're making progress,' I smiled. 'So far, I've been asked to invest some cash into a cloud-based financial solutions service and my first task was to analyse the intended market in Denmark. What I discover is that the market opportunity has two main dimensions.' I write the following on the flipchart:

1. Potential

2. Challenges

'What do you think these will consist of?' I asked them.

'You don't have a crystal ball, so you can't see the future, that's for sure,' Herman remarked, adding, 'Of course, you could quietly slip into the market and begin to make some headway and, before you know it, your growth rate is exponential thanks to word of mouth and reputation. Or you might be lucky and strike gold overnight, but that's unlikely. Forecasting any sort of return based on either of those assumptions would be risky.'

'And foolish,' Freddie added. There was a momentary lull, likely because some of what we were working through was familiar from their not-too-distant past. I break the lull, 'I'm looking at questionable opportunities where the challenge is big and the potential is low. I need to understand three main things,' I said, turning back to the flipchart to write:

- Market size

- Financial viability

- Time to revenue

'If I give my friend $50k, I want to know when I will get my money back. Will that be in two years, twenty years, or never? How much money do I stand to make? What's my best option if I decide to proceed?'

'Assuming you've identified that there's a market opportunity for the potential product fit, then you approach it with a lean mindset as a start-up, utilising continuous discovery and validation,' Sabine stated.

'Which means looking at this cloud-based service as a product and allowing it to develop through the three main product lifecycles,' Leon added.

'You bring together a product team that includes software developers, engineers and sales and marketing,' Freddie said.

Christoph pitched in: 'You spend a few days work-shopping the business model and –' I interrupted Christoph, quickly clarifying, 'As a draft version. Everything is a draft in a lean start-up. Never take anything as final.' Christoph nodded his under-standing and continued, 'You then build the business model.'

'What does that look like, based on how I've described the potential business?' I asked them.

Herman was first to jump in: 'I was going to suggest it was two-sided, made up of SMEs[10] wanting a one-stop solution for their financial software needs on the one hand, and their clients on the other, but actually I think it's just the one model.'

'Why?' I asked.

'Because ultimately, it's the SMEs paying to use the product. Then, I guess, you test the model based on your assumptions from your market research.'

'What does that look like?' I pressed him further.

'You have your north star metrics, which set your growth direction.'

'What is the most important thing I'm measuring?' I interrogated him further.

'The outcome metrics,' he responded.

---

10 Small and medium-sized enterprises

'Although you can't directly influence these metrics,' I explained. 'You need to understand how your business works to monitor all these metrics on a daily basis. You can then determine ways to continuously improve your product, with set goals and where everybody is aligned to the company strategy and focused on the same outcome.'

'Which, in the initial stages, is building and releasing a limited prototype to market, ready to take on board customer feedback,' Herman said.

'I wouldn't go into fully fledged production at this stage, not even after these workshops,' Leon said. 'We did that when we introduced a new credit service into a territory that just wasn't ready for it. They liked the idea of a credit facility, our research told us that, but not the facility we provided them with.'

'We lost a fair amount extracting ourselves from that agreement, too,' Freddie said, with no hint of schadenfreude. It seemed the whole room was complicit in that error of judgement.

'We won't make that mistake again,' Christoph said cheerfully, lifting the mood, 'because next time we'll have fast and cost-efficient ways to validate the product as it develops. That's how we start discovering the business model.'

'The next step being to evaluate how much money we'll make and how quickly,' Leon said.

'We'd need to analyse the financial viability in that case,' Jonas noted, 'identifying when it would break even and at what point it would realise the ROI.'

'And to what level, of course,' Freddie added.

'Which is when you return to the Business Model Canvas,' I said, 'and use it to enter your variable base projections – where the positives and negatives are. That's when you see the potential outcomes of the 50k investment.'

Pulling up the Business Model Canvas graphic once more, I pointed out, 'You can see clearly that the cost of development is always variable. How much will it take to acquire 1,000 customers, or 10,000 customers? Add to that, what's the basket size? How often does the customer buy and what's the retention? These variables are the important numbers, not how much it costs.'

'As you said, the focus is on outcomes, not output,' Christoph confirmed.

'Everything delivered in each one of the product releases, therefore, must be linked to an outcome,' I agreed. 'It's not based on wishful thinking. It's the combined result of a team effort in continuous delivery and continuous discovery.'

'You make it sound so easy,' Christoph remarked, leaning back in his seat.

'I wouldn't say the process itself is easy, but under-standing the process and how it all fits together is better than not following it and then trying to unravel the mistakes.'

'We've all been there in the last couple of years,' Herman lamented.

As the session drew to a close, I briefly mentioned that product discovery directly feeds innovation and told them, 'When I come to explain Google Sprint in part three of the organisational mastery session, you'll see why it's the perfect tool to validate much of the development undertaken during product discovery.'

'What I don't fully understand,' Jonas said, 'is that, yes, I get that we believed we were already moving towards Agile, or at least implementing certain parts of it –'

'That we've pretty much discarded because none of us could see how it linked to the bigger picture,' Freddie interjected. Leon looked disheartened, 'I honestly thought that some of it had stuck and we were doing it right.'

'Like what?' Freddie asked.

'For instance,' Leon responded, 'we still do some digital product discovery.'

'Set up as a project, though,' Christoph identified.

'Agreed, our focus was skewed in the wrong direction in that respect,' Leon continued, 'but we still do design sprints when we start new projects.'

'Incorporating design sprints into your product development process is a good starting point, but it's definitely a long way from digital product discovery,' I explained. 'Some tasks will require a few days to develop and test, but for others it may be several weeks, during which time you'll be receiving feedback from customers on your prototype product.'

'That extended sprint creates the space for ongoing innovation,' Leon observed.

'Correct,' I confirmed, 'and this is where many teams I've taught have said they struggle: putting in place an effective discovery process.'

'That sounds like me and my team,' Jonas said, 'but I'm curious about what we're doing wrong. Which piece of the puzzle is missing?'

'That's a great question. If you think back to what we discussed earlier about how FSS spends so much of its time and resources on customising its products, you're trying to reinvent the wheel every week or exploring random options in the hope that one of them works.'

'Which often it doesn't,' Jonas admitted.

'I imagine that leads to all sorts of frustrations in the team and distrust between stakeholders,' I observed.

'Which is why we need to invest more of our efforts and resources into the design sprint,' Herman noted.

'It gives you space to breathe and develop ideas from concept to prototype. It would be naïve to think that could all happen in five days,' I said.

'You see, I get it now, Herman,' Freddie said. 'If we continuously explore products and release these to market, take customer feedback and use it to adapt the product, revenues will surely increase? We're also staying a step ahead of our competitors.'

'It's the accelerator we've been lacking,' Herman added, 'That's a massive shift in our mindset and operations.'

'Correct,' I confirmed, 'and this is one of the biggest advantages of refocusing your efforts on product, as opposed to projects, because continuous discovery in real market time with your customers at the heart of the evaluation chain will lead to more successful commercial outcomes.'

'Instead of untested projects forcing us back to the drawing board to start the whole cycle again, but still with the same uncertainty,' Leon added. There was a sense of unanimous understanding and agreement in the room.

'Moving on, we'll now work through the three elements of organisational mastery,' I said. 'This is the glue that holds everything together. It's where you'll see how all the sessions we've worked through so far and the knowledge you've gained tie into each other in the big blueprint.'

'Where we'll build on the process of discovery?' Leon asked.

'Yes,' I said, 'and translate that into continuously delivering product to the marketplace. It's the moment you put your foot on the gas pedal and start to drive the business faster, ahead of its competitors.'

I sensed a real buzz of anticipation. I often observe this moment in workshops, when the mood and the body language of everyone in the room lifts, the participants alert and engaged. I attribute it to the fact that nobody feels threatened anymore, worried that they're about to lose their position or authority. They're all on the same page. The executive leadership team has coalesced and knows they're dependent on their collective knowledge and expertise if they are to bring about the digital transformation they need in order to win.

142

THE ADAPT METHODOLOGY™
PROJECT TO PRODUCT SCORECARD

Six sessions completed. Evaluate whether you are leading an outdated project-centric business or a modern product-led company at: https://bit.ly/Scorecard_ProductFirst_Book

7

Organisational Mastery – Part One

Throughout my career, I've engaged with executive leaders and entrepreneurs to understand the main problems they've faced when trying to design, build and grow a company fit for the digital era. Over the course of these conversations, it's become clear to me that there are five common issues that they struggle with and those are how to:

1. Translate strategy into daily operations

2. Reduce time to market

3. Drive continuous improvement

4. Create a learning organisation

5. Drive innovation

On that basis I created and developed the 'organisational mastery' (OM) concept, which is essentially a blueprint for how to create a structure that will help organisations become faster, more effective and more efficient as 'product first' companies in the digital era. Organisational mastery allows a business to maximise its ROI by refocusing its efforts into products, not projects. That requires each product being supported by the right people all in one place to see its development through.

Day Three

Before I had the chance to open the first of the three sessions we would be doing on OM, Herman made an announcement.

'Luis and I talked overnight, and it's become abundantly clear to me that all of us in the executive team are part of the problem, but on the flip side, we can also all be part of the solution – if we work together.'

'Agreed,' Freddie said, nodding.

Looking at each of his colleagues around the table in turn, Herman continued, 'I'm not here as the head honcho because, in reality, that title exists only on paper. I'm here as part of a team, as I think you all are, too. This isn't just about a business I began fifteen years ago, one that, over time, together we've built to become a market leader. The truth is, our successes, exceptional as they are, are behind us. This is about looking forward to the next fifteen years and asking ourselves: where are we heading? Can we survive? Can we continue making a success of what we do? That's why I asked Luis to lead this workshop. I'm not saying I don't still have questions, or concerns about how we can meet these challenges, but I'm keen to turn my curiosity into action and to be seen doing so.'

There was a general hum of agreement. Rousing as Herman's speech was, it was also important in another way: it told not only me, but everyone in the room, that consensus is as vital as the need to question and challenge. These are essential stepping-stones in any learning journey, which required a frank, open and honest discussion about the need for change, which can often feel alien or frightening when compared to established, familiar practices.

This renewed energy was well-timed, as I was about to challenge their preconceptions about OKRs. A common mistake I see is that, while leaders will create a series of OKRs, they are created for teams based in separate departments.

'We're very familiar with OKRs here,' Freddie noted upon reading the new heading on the flipchart. 'In fact, they underpin every project we undertake and help to focus the teams.'

'The problem with that approach,' I challenged him, 'is that nothing really changes as a result.'

'Why?' Herman pressed me.

'Because it reinforces the silo culture and is entirely project focused,' I replied.

'But that's what we do here,' Freddie said. 'We apply Scrum design thinking combined with lean start-up approaches to projects. We've spent thousands on this, bringing in "experts" like yourself every end of year, but...' he paused for a moment, considering his next words, 'I'm guessing from what I've heard so far, that our focus should be on product first, and not be so project-driven?'

'Correct,' I confirmed. 'Instead, what we want is OKRs where the customer is the central focus. That then forces the company to create OKRs aimed at the product in its entirety, breaking down the barriers between silos and their dependencies. With a project-delivery mentality, product becomes a secondary objective almost by default.'

'And as a result, we lose sight of the customer,' Sabine observed, 'since those projects are stuck in their departmental lines, such as marketing, finance, product development, etc.'

'I can see how the pillars of your methodology are beginning to intersect, in which case I'm curious to know how we can improve upon Agile in any significant way,' Freddie said, sitting back in his seat. Freddie's curiosity was in itself a significant step change in his attitude compared to when we first met. It was obvious that the rest of the room were more relaxed as a result of Freddie's increasing buy-in over the last twenty-four hours because this allowed them to give more attention to the workshop and less to dealing with interpersonal issues. This, I suspected, had long been a cause of some aggravation within the business, not wholly due to Freddie, but because the organisation operated along territorial lines.

'Everything you've told me so far,' I continued, 'suggests that FSS still defaults to a pre-digital era management style, in which it measures objectives to connect different operations to its overall strategy. Yes, you might employ Scrum and all the other sexy elements of Agile, because digital businesses are led to believe that's the panacea that will lead to maximum productivity, but without total organisational mastery, and with the current structure of FSS, that approach completely obliterates each department's view of the rest of the business. What's more, that silo approach completely ignores the customer's point of view.'

'Which is where our business should ultimately be focused,' Sabine said. 'We all thought that's where our focus was, but we've fallen down the rabbit hole you've described of developing projects within our individual spheres of operation.'

'We've taken our eye off the main prize: the customer,' Christoph added, 'by not developing product from their point of view.'

'Precisely,' I said, 'which is why it's important to recalibrate your approach to OKRs. It's a subtle but significant shift.'

Jonas still had a quizzical look. I wanted to know more of what he was thinking before we began, so

I asked them all, 'Are there any questions? Do you have any concerns you'd like to raise before we move on?'

As I expected, Jonas shifted a little in his seat, twirling his pen between his fingers, his gaze fixed on the table. He paused, looked up and said, 'I don't want to put a fly into the ointment, but...' He hesitated. We all looked at him expectantly. Generally, Jonas was softly spoken, but still someone who could command authority when he needed to. Whatever it was he had to say, I expected it was based on carefully considered reasoning. I gave him the space to find his words.

Eventually, he said, 'You've outlined what Agility really means and how it relates to the practical implementation of product and product discovery, which leads me to assume this requires us to make some fundamental structural changes to our organisation.'

'Correct,' I said.

'In that case,' Jonas continued, 'how can we build an organisation that will grow and scale at a fast pace, without it becoming overly complex?'

'That's a great question,' I said, but Jonas wasn't finished yet.

He continued, 'I get everything you've shown us so far, and it all makes sense. But one thing's been troubling me all through the break: how do we feed all the necessary work to the teams? How do we structure the company to meet these demands? How do we ensure that the vision translates into the team's backlogs? I'm sorry, Luis, I'm not confused, I just need clarification.'

I'm always happy when questions like these arise. Part of any effort to effect major and complex change in any organisation is first winning the engagement of the people responsible for carrying it out. Jonas was definitely engaged.

'Again, great points, Jonas, but tell me, at this stage, what's your biggest concern? Perhaps I can address that first,' I offered.

'Change will affect what all of us do,' Jonas continued in a measured tone, 'I'm not saying that's a bad thing. I'm totally on board and want to help the business make the necessary transition, but the cost of losing my team as the well-defined unit it is now, feels counterintuitive. I'm not sure how and where I could lead them.'

'What if your leadership could be applied in different areas?' I suggested.

Jonas paused for a moment, then said, 'I guess, on the positive front, if I can personally and professionally contribute to this organisational transformation across different areas where my leadership is valuable, maybe I'll learn something new.'

I was pleased with Jonas' response. For one thing, in voicing his thoughts he may well have echoed those of his colleagues. That he could begin to imagine a positive outcome of a change that would directly affect his leadership role was a big step forward. The impact this would have on the others was tremendously powerful.

'I realise that what I'm about to propose is a lot to take on board. You've each become accustomed to leading your departments and teams based on well-established principles that have stood this business in good stead for many years. Its success speaks for itself, but to survive in the digital era, you've all acknowledged that change is necessary, which means FSS needs to adapt. The next three sessions will focus on understanding the foundations of organisational mastery, which will give you the tools to achieve that.'

'OK, quick question,' Freddie said, 'what you define and what we understand by organisational mastery are obviously two different things, yes?'

Jonas also looked puzzled and asked, 'You've taken us through four of the five pillars of your methodology, why interrupt the flow with organisational mastery? Why isn't that your starting point? Now we know we need to be more aligned as a team and focus on product, how does organisational mastery impact that?'

I turned to the flipchart and, on a clean sheet, wrote up and briefly explained each of the five components of OM.

1. Translate strategy into daily operations

'As an organisation starts to grow, it needs to find effective ways to align everyone within the company. Many leaders find it difficult to create effective ways to translate their strategy into daily operational actions and to measure their impact on delivery. I will show you a new way of using OKRs to set goals that allow you to connect strategy with execution and enable decentralisation and leadership at all levels of the organisation.'

2. Reduce time to market

'When you optimise your processes to release products more rapidly to market, you have a much higher chance of standing out and beating your competitors. That means digital businesses need to fully understand how to implement CoD tools so that they can optimise for speed and not for cost, as traditional companies do.'

3. Continuous improvement

'Embedding a continuous innovation culture among all staff members is crucial to keep pace with a dynamic and ever-changing society. The only way to survive is to continue improving your organisation through innovation and change processes. But as the structures start to grow, you need to have a proper mechanism in place to enable everyone in the organisation to identify and solve problems. I will introduce you to the Organisational Impediments Board, which contains the Agile Improvement Backlog that you can use to discover areas that are blocking and impeding the business.'

4. Create a learning organisation

'Without a proper strategy in place to share knowledge among employees, companies have a higher chance of failure. At the heart of every business is its people and through establishing communities of practice, you have at your disposal a fantastic tool to promote problem solving, knowledge sharing and efficient use of resources, all of which are critical to professional learning.'

5. Drive innovation

'It's essential that organisations continuously enable innovation to flourish at all levels of the business. I'll show you how design thinking is more than just solving a problem; it's also about finding better ways of carrying out tasks and achieving objectives by going beyond conventional means to find a new solution to an old dilemma.

These five components contain the tools that are key to switching your business from being project-led to product-focused. This ultimately leads to enhanced productivity and a greater ROI. Had I begun discussing organisational mastery before your mindset had shifted from project to product, this session would be a much harder sell.'

The room broke into a collective laugh and even Jonas smiled. We were ready to get started with a deep dive into the five components of OM.

OM Component 1: OKRs

'When implemented as a fundamental tenet of a business's operation, OKRs are key to aligning the entire organisation and translating strategy into reality,' I began.

'OKRs from the customer point of view?' Sabine checked.

'Correct,' I confirmed, 'knowing what their pain points are and solving them.'

'Through product discovery and continuous improvement,' Christoph added.

'Yes,' I said, 'and that pivot in approach leads to a move away from project-led initiatives to prioritising product first, which then creates the value streams.'

'Populated with products, as a result of continuous discovery and continual improvement,' Leon added.

'When an organisation embeds that as its principal path, then its entire structure is designed around products that solve customer problems,' I said. 'Waiting a whole year to measure whether you've hit your objectives just doesn't make sense when the world around you is dictated by speed. Why wait, as you do in Waterfall, no matter how much Agile has been implemented in the process?'

'Ah,' was all Freddie could muster. But it was significant all the same.

'Where do we change that?' Herman asked, his eyes boring into me.

I tapped my temples and said, 'First, here. It's like turning a ship around.'

This was my cue to play the room a short video[11] of Captain David Marquet's talk on greatness, based on his book, *Turn The Ship Around!*[12] I, like many, have been inspired by the leadership epiphany he had when, as a newly appointed captain of the USS Santa Fe (a nuclear-powered submarine), Marquet led a large crew hundreds of metres below the surface of the sea, a situation in which there was little room for error. He soon discovered that the crew lacked morale, were performing poorly and had the worst retention in the fleet. On one occasion, Marquet unwittingly issued an impossible order that his crew attempted to follow without question, on the basis that 'you told us to'. Marquet suddenly realised he was heading a 'leader–follower' culture that could present real danger if left unchallenged. Marquet took matters into his own hands and pushed for leadership at every level by instead encouraging a 'leader–leader' culture, one that maximises an individual's potential while reducing dependency on a single leader.

'It's an approach that is shown to deliver sustained performance,' I explained, 'and it's a model that can be applied to any organisation, at any leadership level. Apply this to OKRs and the results are transformative. It not only allows senior leaders to unlock the potential of their people, but it also encourages the exec team to let go. It's a simple, yet powerful representation of how OKRs should be managed.' I could

---

11 'MindSpring Presents: "Greatness" by David Marquet', MindSpring, www.youtube.com/watch?v=OqmdLcyES_Q, accessed November 2022

12 D Marquet, *Turn the Ship Around!* (Penguin, 2013)

see the message hit home and invited the team to respond with their own reflections.

'In that case, it's up to us to provide intent and then hand over control,' said Sabine.

'But first,' Herman interjected, 'we need to make sure we have the correct and competent team members in place to carry out the task.'

'With clarity on where to head from the outset,' Christoph remarked. I nodded; he was correct.

'Which suggests the greater authority resides where the information sits. That's where we create leaders to implement the task at hand,' Freddie added.

Turning back to the flipchart, I summarised the four key points:

1. Provide intent

2. Give control having ensured competence

3. Move authority to where the information is

4. Create leaders

'I always believed that OKRs were tied directly into managing projects,' Jonas observed, 'and then I thought, "no, Luis is trying to steer us in a different direction, toward thinking about product", but actually, this is also about a style of leadership, even before we get to thinking about product.'

'Less top–down, I'm assuming?' Freddie observed.

'Exactly,' I said. 'It's about embracing a mindset that's not authoritarian, which issues commands without considering clarity and competency.'

At this point in my workshops, I like to reference Ben Lamorte, who co-authored the first in-depth reference guide on OKRs, in which he describes them as:

'a critical thinking framework and ongoing discipline that seek to ensure employees work together, focusing their efforts to make measurable contributions that drive the company forward.'[13]

'As a business tool, OKRs have been around longer than most people realise.[14] When they were introduced in Google, they helped transform its business model to make it the outstanding success it is today, as the next slide shows.' I pulled up the following image, showing the origins and evolution of the OKR framework.

---

13   PR Niven and B Lamorte, *Objectives and Key Results: Driving Focus, Alignment, and Engagement* (Wiley, 2016)

14   OKRs as a business tool have been in existence since the 1970s. They first materialised under Andy Grove, the founder of the Intel Create OKR framework, and John Doerr, who later wrote the bestseller *Measure What Matters*. In this book, Doerr explains how he learned everything he knew about OKRs from Intel and then in 1999 introduced them into Google when he became an early investor. The subsequent meteoric success of Google helped make OKRs so widely used and since then everyone has wanted to use OKRs. If only they knew the other part of the puzzle. The problem is that the power of OKRs is often lost in age-old corporate practices that swallow and de-validate their immense usefulness to the point that any benefits to be gained from implementing Agile are rendered non-existent.

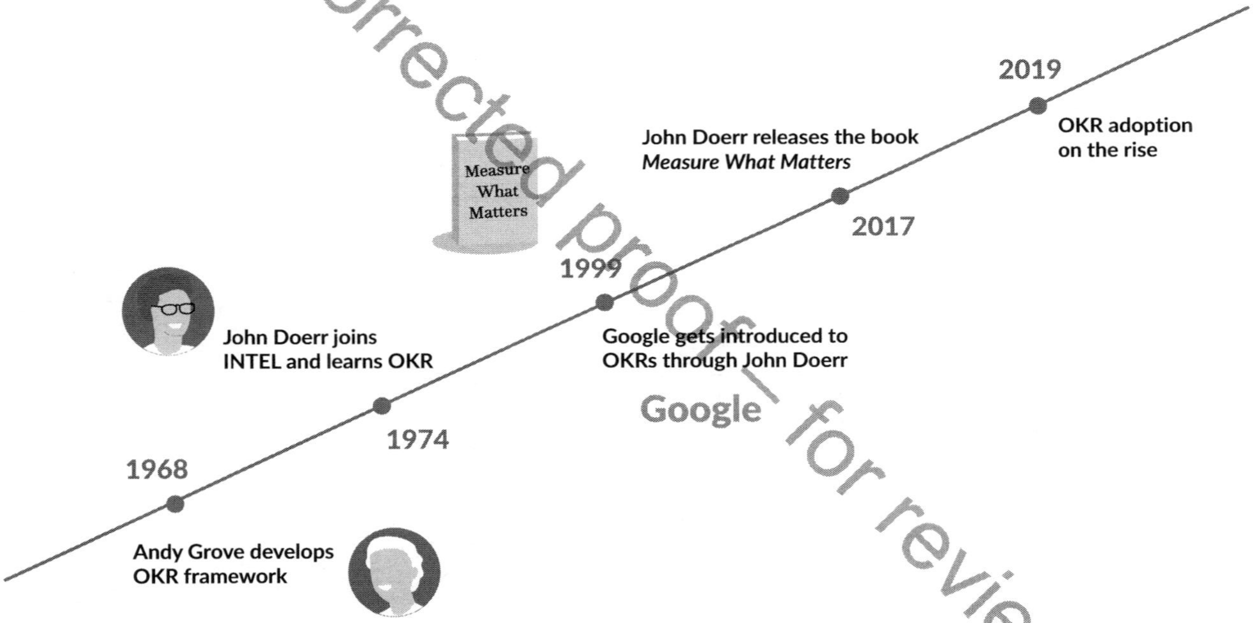
Measure What Matters
1968
Andy Grove develops OKR framework
1974
John Doerr joins INTEL and learns OKR
1999
Google gets introduced to OKRs through John Doerr
Google
2017
John Doerr releases the book *Measure What Matters*
2019
OKR adoption on the rise

Evolution of OKRs

'Principally, OKRs are designed to solve problems from a customer point of view and to create the right product to do that,' I explained to the group. 'To do this, though, the skill set to develop that product needs to be in place from day one. A smart organisation will identify the people in the business best placed to deliver the OKRs that link directly to the product value stream.'

Herman leaned forward, looking at Freddie, and said: 'We need to rethink, don't we? It can no longer be the case that we respond to a sales or marketing brief and attempt to create a product from a project. Especially one that might ultimately fail because it's been developed in isolation.'

'As an IT-led project,' Freddie interjected, 'that then gets shot down in flames six months or a year later because it doesn't deliver what ops or marketing are looking for.'

What could have been a moment of tension was quickly deflected when Christoph chipped in. 'In other words, we're all responsible for solving the problem from the customer point of view. When we run any OKR cycle we shouldn't pigeonhole it as a marketing or an IT OKR, it's a customer problem solving activity.'

'OKRs, therefore, feed directly into value streams. They're not just department-led projects?' Jonas suggested.

I agreed, adding, 'OKRs are designed to tell you what those value streams are and become the tool that translates strategy into daily operations, having a significant impact on how these are then structured.'

'OKRs issued at the top level demand that you have a clear objective, or vision of where you want to go and that you understand the need to create clear objectives from the bottom level up to achieve it,' I said. 'It's just like turning the ship around. The teams below get to define their lower-level objectives based on the clarity of the top-level objective. This is communicated throughout the organisation to ensure complete alignment.'

'Do we need an OKR coach to guide us through this?' Christoph suggested.

'Not at all,' I stressed. 'That's the last thing you need.'

'Why?' Christoph looked puzzled.

'OKR coaches don't have a clue how to set up organisations,' I explained. 'They will just give you more consultants who mill around and annoy your people. All they can tell you is how the tools work; they won't help you build a digital product organisation.'

'We need to know how these tools work, though, don't we?' Christoph pressed me.

'Not from a consultant's point of view, no. They're not interested in how you intend for your organisation to operate, so they will simply view OKRs from department A or department B's point of view, which perpetuates that silo mentality that you want to dismantle. Our aim here is to build a digital product company and to ensure that the OKRs are fully aligned and integrated with your entire product development cycle. Then your OKRs will be written from the point of view of the customer and compel you to create the requisite value streams. That then helps to define the organisational structure, which is what's needed for organisational mastery and transformation to happen. In my experience, 99% of OKR consultants won't do that.'

'To summarise,' I said, 'OKRs support clearer and more direct means of communication. They also demand laser-like focus – best practice tells us that we can only have five OKRs. Transparency, from the CEO to the shop floor, is key if the whole organisation is to completely align to the objective. It's good practice to build OKRs on a quarterly basis so that they can be aligned with the quarterly results. Agility, in this context, allows you to shift direction every three months. Engagement increases because everyone is involved in working out how to achieve the results; it's not just a prescriptive directive from the boss. Finally, where there is visionary thinking, there comes the challenge of trying to create aspirational objectives that encourage everyone to go the extra mile.'

As I finished speaking, I pulled up a summary of the OKR framework.

Looking at it, Freddie concluded, 'The solution is to build OKRs from the customer point of view – or, to put it another way, from the product point of view.'

'That's it,' I confirmed. 'Your OKR framework then fits into that, guided by the four values of...' I write on the flipchart:

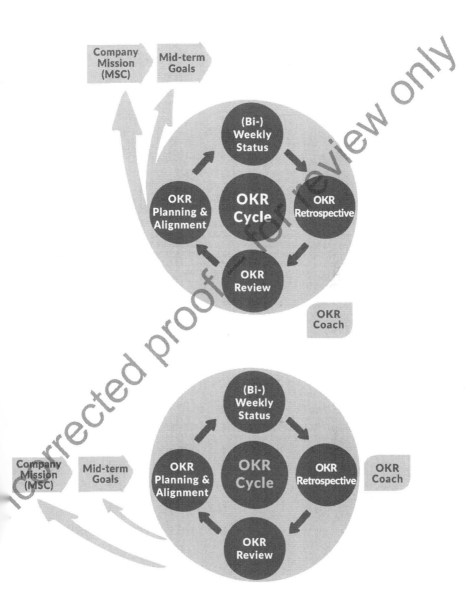

The OKR Framework

- Values alignment

- Transparency

- Commitment

- Intrinsic motivation

'These principles are underpinned by…' I write underneath:

- Self-organising teams

- Short iterations

- Focus

- And continuous improvement

'What's the typical timeframe to turn this around?' Leon asked.

'Different goals can have different timeframes. For example, tactical goals tend to change faster than strategic goals, so OKRs can separate tactics and strategies by utilising a nested model,' I explained.

An example of the different timeframes of cascading goals might look something like this:

- Within three to five years – the long-term strategic vision.

- Within twelve months – annual strategic OKRs, which will be used by the whole company.

- Within three months – quarterly tactical goals for teams, coupled with a mid-quarter review.

- Within two weeks – bi-weekly check-ins to track results.

'Then what?' Jonas asked.

'At the end of each cycle, there's a retrospective exercise that mirrors and compares to the goals set out at the beginning of the process. Nothing is left to chance and there's no "wait and see". In this way, OKRs demonstrate their super-efficacy and impact, not just on how a business grows and develops, but also on the people who work within it. You can see this when you look at the Vision Pyramid.' I showed them the next diagram.

The Vision Pyramid

The Vision Pyramid shows the journey toward achieving the big picture strategic goal, which can span anything from three to ten years. Along the way are the mid-term goals and the company OKRs that cascade into the rest of the organisation over each three-monthly cycle.

'This,' I explain, 'is one component of organisational mastery. Once you implement it, it will transform how your organisation operates.'

'That looks quite different to any plan we've worked from,' Herman observed.

'It will be,' I agreed, 'because it's the complete antithesis to traditional structures and how the strategic vision is typically achieved. Here you have the strategy, then each product has its own set of OKRs organised like start-ups that rely on planning. That planning is then aligned with everyone in the organisation. It's a daily cycle that pulses the life blood of the business into all your products through bi-weekly check-ins to ensure there are no glitches or major hurdles. If there are, they get dealt with straight away. The difference between this implementation of Agile and others that you may be familiar with, is that it *all* connects, across the whole organisation.'

This slide, the big reveal, can have a mesmeric effect. It seemed to be working its magic on the group at FSS.

'Everyone understands how their work connects to the big picture and so what they do actually impacts the company vision.'

I paused for breath so that the room could take in what I had said. It was Freddie who broke the silence. 'I'm prepared to admit that I never really understood the point of Agile, not to the extent that you're laying out today. I don't know if I'm speaking for all of us, but it's becoming much clearer to me why I've had a long-standing problem with OKRs and the endless consultants walking through our doors. Maybe we – and by that I mean "I" – have just been out of sync the whole time?'

I have to confess that in moments such as this I experience a quiet elation, a sense of pure job satisfaction. If I have a calling, it is this: to help C-suite leaders extract themselves from deeply entrenched business practices that are the result of years of conformity, practices that have been bludgeoned into them from an early age, tracing right back to the roots of their education. The post-industrial revolution and early twentieth-century business philosophies were founded upon the principles of top–down, silo-led structures that inevitably create barriers and provoke conflict between departments. This is endemic in countless organisations, many of which have fallen from the lofty heights, or have imploded completely. Survival is not an entitlement. In the digital era, knowing what you need to do, how you need to change, to survive is key. Embracing radical change and implementing it across an entire organisation takes courage translated into action. When Freddie admitted for the first time that his perspective and practices needed to change, this took courage. It also showed that he was willing to be part of a collective leadership endeavour to bring that change about.

I could sense huge relief in Herman, not only because it was clear that Freddie was willing to be part of the solution, but also perhaps because Herman had inwardly acknowledged that he had also been part of the problem. We broke for ten minutes for coffee.

THE ADAPT METHODOLOGY™ PROJECT TO PRODUCT SCORECARD

Seven sessions completed. Evaluate whether you are leading an outdated project-centric business or a modern product-led company at: https://bit.ly/Scorecard_ProductFirst_Book

8

Organisational Mastery – Part Two

Following a short break, we all gathered back in the boardroom. The three-part OM session is intense, but this is necessary to gather and harness momentum as participants begin to realise that the ADAPT Methodology™ is a blueprint for connecting an entire organisation in everything it does, from the leadership team to the frontline employees. Having challenged their thinking, it was time to take them to the next level.

OM Component 2: Cost of Delay

Most companies run a number of projects in tandem; knowing which they should prioritise can prove tricky. Cost of Delay (CoD) is a concept that helps executive leaders determine which initiatives should be given a higher priority, which allows them to obtain the highest ROI from their product portfolio. I was about to outline to Herman and his colleagues a tool that would help them better understand the impact of time on a projected result by calculating and comparing the cost of not finishing a project, or feature, and opting to do it later. In short, it highlights the loss or postponement of a benefit, or value, because of a delay.

Whenever I introduce CoD in workshops, I'm met with a sense of disbelief, coupled with a certain degree of anger that for years organisations have been leaking money into a bottomless pit. FSS was no different in that respect, especially when I set them the task of working out a ballpark figure for themselves. First, I asked a simple question: 'How long does it take to get anything over the line in this organisation?' This was met with knowing laughter and Freddie replied, 'A long time – and I mean a *long* time.'

'You're in good company,' I replied, 'since that's the same for most organisations. The irony is, it's not because the actions themselves take a long time; it's because they get stuck in endless backlogs and queues, waiting for one department to sign one part off so that another can then carry it out. Multiply that several times over for just one action and you can see where the delays come from.'

'The reality is each feature takes a different amount of time to create and implement,' Leon justified.

I nodded my agreement, 'But I'm assuming they don't all carry the same level of worth in the business.

In which case, prioritising one means limiting or delaying the other. Each day a feature isn't in production is another day that the company won't profit from it.'

'That's true,' Sabine said. 'I remember two years ago when we were talking about expansion and wanted to redesign and upgrade our APG[15] product with an opt-in for the US market. We jumped through so many hoops just to get the prototype developed in a user-friendly format. We pinned a lot on that being successful and it took so long to see the light of day.'

'That's the difference in being able to distinguish how valuable something is and how urgent it is. In hindsight, how could that delay have been avoided, so that you could have brought that prototype to the market sooner, where it would've been generating revenue faster?' I asked the room, not singling anyone out.

Leon looked thoughtful and answered, 'Now that, going forward, we'll be thinking about OKRs in the ways you suggested, we could've reduced the time to market if we'd assigned to the APG feature a dedicated team with the requisite skill sets.'

'Agreed,' Freddie said, nodding his head vigorously, before adding, a little defensively, 'For the record, that delay wasn't just down to my department.'

'I know that now,' Sabine replied, 'but I remember at the time I felt so frustrated with your team because it was stuck in your department for over twelve weeks.'

---

15 Automatic payment generator

'That's because I was waiting on a decision being signed off by Christoph,' Freddie retorted.

'How do you think I felt,' Christoph joined in, 'when I couldn't get a response on compliance?'

'Which just goes to prove my point,' I said.

'I think in total it took over forty-six weeks to deliver from the point we agreed on it, thirty-eight of which were down to backlogs and waiting for decisions,' Sabine recalled.

'That sounds fairly typical to me,' I said. 'In my experience, it's not usual for the waiting time to be in excess of 80% of the total time taken. Which is crazy, especially having invested so much time and effort into identifying your value streams and developing product as a result. Agile is brilliant at accelerating value, but CoD can wipe out all of those benefits if allowed to remain unchecked.'

'When you say "unchecked"…?' Herman asked.

'Identifying which products and features will bring in the most revenue quickest, and the cost of a delay in getting them to market, can be significant. A CoD analysis identifies which of your product features will have the greatest impact – it's those that need to be prioritised.'

'Do we not do that already?' Herman asked, looking around the table, but being met with blank faces.

'That you need to ask that is also part of the problem,' I said bluntly. 'It's not just FSS; most organisations are completely blind to backlogs in their end-to-end process. And because they're "Agile" – or

believe they are – they'll focus on the individual effi-
ciencies within those processes rather than the whole
system that is needed to deliver value. If they only
knew what that cost of delay meant in real terms,
they'd be less blind to it.'

'I guess we've just never connected urgency and
value in that way?' Herman mused.

'That needs to change,' I said. 'For every week's
delay when a new product or feature could be generating, for example, $200k, then over 38 weeks that
would amount to lost revenue totalling $8 million.'

There was a collective sharp intake of breath
around the table. When CoD is spelled out in raw,
hard figures, it often takes people's breath away.

'In which case, we all need to make better decisions,' Freddie said.

'And we need to understand the value of what
we're working on,' Sabine agreed.

'You also need to know that this approach offers
the business even greater flexibility to develop and
release new product to the market when conditions
demand it,' I said.

'How's that possible,' Leon asked, 'if we're already
tied into OKRs on quarterly cycles?'

'Every quarter the company has the flexibility to
adapt,' I explained. 'Meaning that if you need to kill,
or pause, a product development you can. Nobody
knows what's around the corner and sometimes
events are outside of everyone's control, but that
doesn't mean the only option is to stop and stand still.
One of my digital banking clients had been devel-

oping a consumer bill-split app just as the Covid-19 pandemic hit. The whole world was in lockdown, so no one was out at restaurants and bars. This client made an OKR that redeployed the entire workforce to create a product that enabled consumers to make payments to a gaming platform that was a previously unavailable feature. With the world now confined and looking to widen their at-home leisure pursuits, the fast roll-out of a payment app within that quarterly cycle provided a much-needed solution to a customer problem. In the process, the client also acquired 33% more new customers. If the client had remained stuck in their traditional ways, they may have continued developing a product that there was simply no market for. With flexibility that the OKRs provided and dedicated product teams in place, they were able to prioritise one feature over another. In this case, the CoD for the gaming app payment feature was significantly more than the bill-split app and they were able to shift focus to the more urgent product.'

Understanding CoD can help in three ways, which I wrote up on the flipchart:

- Decision making – the economic trade-offs are visible. The value of speed over efficiency is then easy to understand.

- Prioritisation – by using CD3[16] you deliver more total value for a given capacity.

---

16 Cost of Delay divided by duration – more on this later

- Focus – changes from dates and cost estimates to speed and value.

'Ultimately, this is about value and urgency,' I explained. 'You can look at it through a qualitative filter, but it's better when you attach real numbers to it.'

'I'll say so,' agreed Herman. 'I hate to think just how much we've let slip through our fingers over time.'

'In future, to focus your thoughts better, all cost or value decisions the company makes can be put into one of four categories,' I said, writing the below up on the flipchart.

Does the decision, action or activity:

1. Increase revenue? When you don't release a new product/feature into the market, you lose opportunities to make money.

2. Protect revenue? Each week a product stays out of the market, customers will turn to your competitors, which means lost revenue.

3. Reduce costs? Each opportunity to implement automation that is lost results in unnecessary and costly manual work.

4. Avoid costs? For example, you should always maintain regulatory compliance in all the territories you market in to avoid financial penalties.

Cost/Value Framework

Increase revenue	Increasing sales to new or existing customers. Delighting or disrupting to increase market share and size.
Protect revenue	Improvements and incremental innovation to sustain current market share and revenue figures.
Reduce costs	Costs that we are currently incurring, that can be reduced. More efficient, improved margin or contribution.
Avoid costs	Improvements to sustain current cost base. Costs we are not currently incurring but may do in the future.

Freddie was quick to observe, 'Each of those categories relates to money – either to be gained, or lost, depending on the decisions we make around CoD.'

'Correct,' I confirmed, 'but those decisions will be better informed because, as you will see in the next three slides, you'll have a better understanding of the value versus the urgency, which will help you prioritise.'

Urgency profiles

'Next, I'm going to explain how the effect of delay differs depending on the potential benefits,' I told them.

'How can there be any benefit to delaying going to market,' Jonas asked, 'if you're describing losing money by doing so?'

'You need to base that decision on the wider market influences and conditions,' I explained. Generally, the two main variables to consider when analysing the cost versus the benefit of delay are:

1. The length of the benefits lifecycle (how quickly the benefits ramp up and down)

2. Whether or not the peak of demand is affected by delay

'In other words,' Freddie said, 'if we want to understand the urgency of an idea, new or old, we also need to understand the lifecycle of its benefits.'

'And the effect of delay, in that case,' Herman said. 'I think we're all acutely aware that we've been on the back foot in that regard.'

Silent acknowledgement of Herman's glum words hung in the room as I called up the next example.

Short lifecycle where peak is affected by delay

'Where a product has a short lifecycle, the CoD can be catastrophic to the point of killing it off altogether,' I explained. 'If it can't hit the peak demand, there's little point in releasing it at all, as it will already be obsolete. At best, it may catch up with demand, but a lot of revenue will have been lost due to the delay.'

'What would be a commercial example of that?' Sabine asked.

177

'In gaming, Pro Evolution Soccer usually releases ahead of FIFA. Any delay will cost FIFA revenue and, because the game itself only has a twelve-month shelf-life, it will never catch up.'

'We don't have anything like that here,' Leon said, though he sounded uncertain.

'I wouldn't be so sure,' Freddie mumbled.

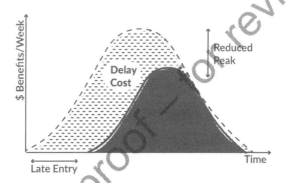

Short Lifecycle – Peak Affected by Delay

Long lifecycle where peak is affected by delay

'Similarly, for long product cycles, the cost of delaying the point of market entry equates to lost revenue,' I said.

'And I presume market share, too?' Christoph asked.

'Especially market share,' I said, 'after which point, trying to catch up is like climbing up a mountain backward with both legs tied together. You'll always be behind the market leaders.'

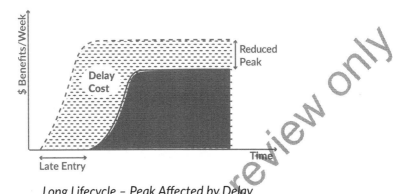

Long Lifecycle – Peak Affected by Delay

Long lifecycle – peak unaffected by delay

'One of the advantages of a monopoly in the market-place is that a business can "afford" the CoD because its customers are ready and waiting to consume its new features or products.'

'Like Apple with the iPhone?' Christoph asked.

'Indeed,' I confirmed. 'Apple has such a strong and defined market position, if it is late to the market with a new feature, the peak remains unaffected since its huge customer base will still almost certainly buy it.'

'Does that mean, if you have a monopoly, there's no chance of losing money with a delay to market?' Sabine asked.

'After all, there's no other iPhone,' Jonas added, 'so if they don't release a new feature to the market, they're not losing anything. Are they?'

'Not true,' I contradicted them, 'because if a company with a monopoly assumes that its customers are guaranteed to buy their products because they're crazy about them, it risks reducing the length of its peak, so that the maximum potential revenue is never fully realised.'

'Something tells me not to think about that time in 2009 when we were dominant in Germany and Austria,' Freddie said, 'and it took 7 months to release our Cash Flow Insights feature. We could've cleaned up sooner. Just like Sabine mentioned with the APG. History repeats itself, over and over in this place.'

'Not anymore,' Herman said with a steely tone.

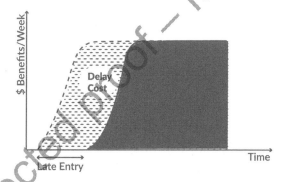

Long Lifecycle – Peak Unaffected by Delay

I looked around the table, everyone seemed to be engaged in private reflection following my CoD presentation. As I mentioned, the moment you can start seeing real figures, the reality begins to bite, and bite hard. I knew that each would be doing some unpleasant sums in their heads right now, because they'd each know that they had contributed to a delay somewhere. Rather than engaging in a blame game, it was becoming apparent to the team that it was the structure of the organisation that was the primary driver of revenue loss, not the people within it. Much of the financial leakage they'd been experiencing was invisible, simply because they'd been looking in the wrong places. It wasn't a design fault, nor a marketing failure that was causing their poor performance, the product and features they'd been turning out were doomed from the start.

I pulled up the following diagram.

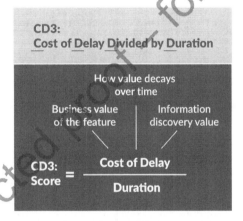

CD3 Explained

'The good news is…' I explained that through correct prioritisation using CD3, or cost of delay divided by duration, much CoD can be avoided by knowing in advance which features will cost more in terms of delay per week so that they can be prioritised in terms of development and release. The trick is to understand the different outcomes depending on the duration of the delay.

I pulled up my example table.

Prioritising with CD3

	Cost of Delay	Duration	CD3 Score
Feature A	$1,000/Week	5 weeks	200
Feature B	$4,000/Week	1 weeks	4,000
Feature C	$5,000/Week	2 weeks	2,500

'It's obvious that Feature C needs prioritising – it's got the highest CoD,' Leon said.

'Not true,' I countered. 'The number you want to look at is the CD3 score – that's the cost per week divided by the duration of the development. It's not always the cost per week that determines the priority. Feature B has a CD3 score of 4,000, which is significantly higher than Feature C with a score of 2,500.'

'I'm not sure I understand,' Leon said, 'because Feature C would cost us $1,000 more than Feature B. What am I missing here?'

'Let's do a quick exercise to help everyone understand it. Based on the figures I've just shown you, I'd like you to calculate the costs of delays in the following scenarios…' I pulled up the next table.

Cost of Delay Exercise – Scenarios

Scenario A	Calculate the total cost of delay if you implement:
	• First Feature A
	• Second Feature B
	• Third Feature C
Scenario B	Calculate the total cost of delay if you implement:
	• First Feature B
	• Second Feature C
	• Third Feature A
Scenario C	Calculate the total cost of delay if you implement:
	• First Feature C
	• Second Feature B
	• Third Feature A

'This isn't going to be as easy as it sounds, is it?' Christoph pondered.

'Tell me in ten minutes,' I said, and left them to make their calculations.

'Okay,' Herman announced when I returned, 'after some intense discussion, we've finally agreed on the costs of delay. At first, we thought they were lower, but then Sabine pointed out we weren't factoring in all the durations concurrently. But we're agreed.'

I smiled broadly, partly in relief that they'd followed the logic, but also because they were correct. Here's how they arrived at the figures:

Scenario A

For the 5 weeks we are working on Feature A we incur Cost of Delay of $(1k+4k+5k)$ per week. Delay Cost = $50,000

For the 1 week we are working on Feature B we incur Cost of Delay of $(4k+5k)$ per week. Delay Cost = $9,000

For the 2 weeks we are working on Feature C we incur Cost of Delay of $5k$ per week. Delay Cost = $10,000

TOTAL COST OF DELAY = $69,000

Scenario B

For the 1 week we are working on Feature B we incur Cost of Delay of $(4k+5k+1k)$ per week. Delay Cost = $10,000

For the 2 weeks we are working on Feature C we incur Cost of Delay of $(5k+1k)$ per week. Delay Cost = $12,000

For the 5 weeks we are working on Feature A we incur Cost of Delay of $1k$ per week. Delay Cost = $5,000

TOTAL COST OF DELAY = $27,000

Scenario C

For the 2 weeks we are working on Feature C we incur Cost of Delay of $(4k+5k+1k)$ per week. Delay Cost = $20,000

For the 1 week we are working on Feature B we incur Cost of Delay of $(5k+1k) per week. Delay Cost = $5,000

For the 5 weeks we are working on Feature A we incur Cost of Delay of $1k per week. Delay Cost = $5,000

TOTAL COST OF DELAY = $30,000

'Congratulations,' I said. 'It's not as easy as it looks, as Christoph rightly identified. But it's an important exercise to get right, so I'm interested to hear what you'll take away from it.'

'It's been quite a shock to us all,' Herman admitted.

'Why's that?' I asked, though I suspected I knew what he was about to say.

'Because the amount of effort that's needed is the same, but the duration and value are vastly different. It really does all come down to prioritising correctly based on that equation – duration over value. We can see it with our own eyes – the more we prioritise on that basis, the less money we lose, doing the same amount of work. It's $69k for Scenario A, $27k for Scenario B and $30k for Scenario C.'

'How, then, would you summarise this CoD exercise?' I asked.

'May I?' Freddie indicated he wanted to speak for the group and they nodded their consent. 'If we optimise our processes to release products more rapidly to market, this shows that we'll have a better chance of standing out and beating competitors. To do that, being the digital company that we are, we need to design the business around the value streams and, in the process, fully implement these CoD tools so that we can optimise for cost, not speed.'

'As traditional companies do,' Sabine added, 'which is the mistake we've made in our strategic operations.'

'And as you've probably guessed already,' I said, 'based on the numbers, OM will also shape how you budget in the future – so let's talk about lean budgeting.'

Lean budgeting

'Traditionally,' Herman said, 'we've based our budgets on past data.' There were nods of agreement around the table. 'With the lean approach we'll be making more valuable investments having evaluated the CoD.'

'A budget holder then acts more like a venture capital fund holder,' Christoph noted, catching Herman's thinking, 'which means they can take a more diligent and proactive approach to killing bad or less lucrative ideas quickly.'

'We're very traditional, aren't we, in how we allocate budgets against specific projects, considering we're a digital business?' Sabine observed. 'For example, the profitability tracker tool we introduced last year for the construction industry, each of us had responsibility for our own budget.'

'Yes, and what a disaster that was,' Freddie laughed.

'True,' Sabine replied, 'but nobody could know what was around the corner, which had a huge impact on our spend in a sector that was grinding to a halt.'

'That's the problem,' I said, 'and 99.9999% of organisations still manage their budgets in traditional ways. We all know what that looks like – each department is assigned an annual budget to spend on its own activities. More often than not, it's based on an educated guess that results in an underspend, where the rest then needs to be spent before year end on unnecessary items or activities that contribute nothing to overall productivity, ROI or the good of the business. It's money down the drain.'

'That explains Christoph's disco-lit, digitised water fountain,' Jonas joked.

'And the five-star long weekend at the Bavarian lakes for Sabine and her management team,' Leon added.

'This kind of spending may be good for team morale,' I continued, 'but it doesn't contribute toward the growth of the business. I feel confident that, going forward, FSS will sponsor individual OKRs on a quarterly basis that will pay for everything that is required to release a product to the market. It's a highly efficient, flexible and cost-productive way of assigning budget because at the end of each quarterly cycle it can be decided whether to continue sponsoring the product, or kill it if it's not performing, allowing that budget to be re-assigned to the next product development.'

'Sabine,' Freddie turned to her, 'looks like you may have to fund your next trip to the lakes yourself.'

The room broke into laughter, though I'm not sure Sabine shared the amusement. She cut through the laughter and asked: 'Who sponsors the OKR, if not a head of department?'

'The budget is sponsored by the head of the product and, every three months, the product team decides where to best allocate its resources based on its continuous discovery and development.'

Leon raised his hand, looking concerned. 'What if it's not working? That can happen.'

'Of course it can,' I replied. 'The significant difference is that, as the executive, you will be much more involved in the product development, which is intended to solve customers' problems. You'll be able to identify every three months if and how the product aligns with the longer-term strategy, then decide whether to continue or reprioritise. You'll always be the ones, as product owners and/or strategists, with their finger on the pulse, working with a team to translate strategy into operations.'

'The product owners, then, are the more operational part of the team, ensuring that the strategy is implemented in that three-month cycle, while the head of the product is thinking two to five years into the future?' Leon pressed further.

'You won't be losing your job, in that case,' Freddie joked, 'we still need you.'

'This creates huge flexibility for us,' Herman cut in. 'Assuming it allows us to identify our value streams, driven by the OKRs on three monthly cycles, we can decide far more quickly if a product is strategically important enough to continue developing it. If not, we can choose to sponsor a whole new set of OKRs in another product as part of the value stream. It's about what makes sense to the business, decided in real time.'

'Where everyone is aligned to the strategy and clear on what those objectives are, working as a team,' Leon added.

'Luis,' Freddie said, 'I want to apologise. I thought I knew this organisation and how it worked inside out. What you've shown me today is that I barely know it from the outside in.' He approached me and shook my hand. It was an important moment for us all and we took a short break.

OM Component 3: Impediments

Project-led organisations are structured in departmental silos and these create impediments to the rapid progress a business needs to succeed in the digital era. This isn't about diluting anyone's authority or dismissing their expertise; it's about maximising all teams through widening the scope. That's where organisational mastery comes in – it provides the necessary framework. It's the glue that holds the whole organisation together while also creating space for discovery, innovation and growth.

Upon their return, I explained this to the group. 'This is about moving from impediment to improvement then?' Herman asked.

'Yes,' I confirmed, 'and while it does involve some radical changes, those changes won't need to be implemented from day one; they will be introduced over a period of time until the organisation's transformation is complete. Removing those impediments unlocks the transformative process.'

'Easier said than done,' Freddie remarked wryly, 'especially when we've been too busy erecting barriers and protecting departmental territories.'

'That depends on your approach going forward. There will always be problems to tackle and manage; the question is how to address them,' I explained.

'Are you suggesting that organisational impediments will always be at the heart of continuous improvement?' Jonas asked.

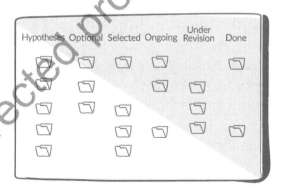

Organisational Impediment Board

'Yes,' I confirmed, pulling up an image of my impediment board, 'because companies have too many organisational problems that sit inside their silos and nobody outside of them knows what they are. That's why

I created the impediment board, as a place where the entire company can make problems visible, which –'

'– Allows others to contribute to solving them?' Christoph finished.

'Yes, because that way, the whole company is always striving for excellence, looking to create new ways to stand out from its competition. Average executives are usually prepared to settle for less. Please, raise your hand if you think of yourself as "average"?' I asked them. Of course, nobody did. 'Does anyone here believe that what isn't broken shouldn't be fixed?'

'That's a trick question,' Freddie observed. 'If you'd asked me that two days ago, I might have said yes,' he smiled shrewdly.

'We all might have,' Sabine said, 'although we didn't actually know what was broken at that time.'

'Hence – to answer your earlier question – why I do this session now,' I said. 'It's clear that FSS, like most organisations, still has the potential and room for growth. How it begins that process is by getting rid of its organisational impediments. Success is no longer measured in how long a company has been in business. A ten-year-old company that learns organisational mastery can achieve what a two-year-old company has in less time.'

'How?' Leon asked.

'Executives who fail to see beyond their horizon will only pull a company down. Your ability to spot room for improvements is essential, but you can't do it alone – you need to be surrounded by people who see the same potential.'

'I think all of us here are on the same page,' Herman said, surveying the room. Everyone nodded in agreement.

'If I were to ask what's been holding the business back, why hasn't it moved forward as quickly as you would like, what would you say?' I asked.

'Given that we've never had an impediment board to refer to, I'd say none of us are aware of each other's departmental problems. It's the old "that's your problem" mentality,' Christoph said, seeming almost embarrassed as he continued. 'If we supported each other more, and if our teams knew they could help one another to solve problems as they arose, we might have avoided so much inter-department aggro in the past. Just knowing they can add the problems to the board, which everyone in the business has open access to and is encouraged to contribute support and solutions, will make a huge difference to the culture – and the outcomes – at FSS.'

'This, Freddie, is where we see Agile in action,' I said smiling broadly at him. 'This contains the Agile improvement backlog. These are the issues that are found to be blocking and impeding an organisation.'

'I should've guessed,' he said, good-humouredly.

'For each of the six columns on the impediment board, you assign Agile managers to handle and solve each of the specified improvements. Their role is critical, since the tasks won't be simple – most of these improvements will likely require profound changes within the organisation.'

'Hmm,' Freddie muttered, his eyes narrowing a little, 'I'm probably still a little sceptical, even though you've done a lot to turn my thinking. Tell me, what exactly will these so-called Agile managers do?'

'Their main responsibility is to remove the topics from the board, but they can only do that by liaising with all parties concerned, everyone from the senior leadership to managerial.'

'I can feel a Kanban board coming along,' Freddie remarked.

'Correct,' I confirmed.

'Looks like I've retained more about Agile than I'd care to admit,' he joked.

'What happens if I identify a problem my team can't fix?' Leon asked.

'Then we'd have an organisational problem,' Herman said.

'We do have an organisational problem,' Freddie noted.

'There's no doubt that organisations often overlook areas that need improvement, but this impedes their growth. Even when they do identify them, they lack the means of bringing transparency to these areas. The impediment board allows teams and individuals to develop possible enhancements and search for ways to improve the whole organisation. Now we're beginning to drill down into the impediments to this, some of which will seem obvious, while others will appear for the first time.'

'Except they've been there all along, hiding in plain sight,' Sabine remarked, 'in which case, how do we spot them?'

'That's the beauty of the impediment board. You create six columns, which look like this…' I wrote on the flipchart a short version of the following:

1. Hypothesis – where possible improvements are expressed as an initial idea, a hypothesis that may, or may not, bring about the desired results. Every decision follows a certain format:

   – Implementing the change

   – Promising to find a solution to the problem

   – Predicting the benefits

   – Identifying the measurement type

2. Options – each hypothesis should have several ways it could be implemented. Teams have a responsibility to find out which option is the easiest to apply and can generate ROI.

3. Selected – the option the team chooses for each hypothesis.

4. Ongoing – the current option being implemented.

5. Review – every option requires review, which includes assessing whether the improvement was implemented successfully and if it brought about the desired result.

6. Done – indicates whether implementing the improvement was successful.

It is essential that this board is visible to everyone within the organisation so that they can see the ongoing improvements and initiatives. The board's visibility and accessibility can have a huge impact on an organisation with amazing results, including:

- Creating transparency

- Enabling continuous improvement

- Allowing managers to execute tasks within the organisational system

- Paving the way toward becoming a learning organisation

'Does the implementation process rely on it being totally Agile?' Freddie asked.

'Yes,' I confirmed.

'All of it?' he presses me further.

'Everything should be implemented in a manner that's deemed Agile. You'll organise a team get-together every two weeks, during which you review what's been achieved and plan what to tackle in the coming weeks.'

'We set meetings all the time, so that shouldn't be difficult,' Christoph remarked, with a hint of sarcasm.

'Then you'll also have a monthly get-together when the team will run an Agile retrospective to analyse the various ways it can improve.'

'So we're constantly monitoring ourselves, not just the improvements and impediments,' Christoph observed, seemingly having a lightbulb moment.

'Meaning each team assumes full ownership of its agenda as well as the outcome. Wow.'

'It's a perfect opportunity for the team to pause and reflect on its work and how it's carried out,' I confirmed.

'Hang on,' Leon interjected, 'who exactly are the team members?'

'The impediment board is owned predominantly by the Agile managers. They're joined in the team by senior managers, one of which may be Scrum master,' I explained.

'Ah, the good old Scrum master,' Freddie smirked.

'Or you could think of them as the team's COO,' I offered.

'Now that, I like the sound of,' he laughed.

'Nobody is left on the side lines – in fact, it's essential that you, as the executive management, are part of the process. Your buy-in and involvement greatly empowers the rest of the organisation, which can drive its own improvements.'

'Such as?' Herman asks.

'It means that anybody in the chain of command feels they will be heard by the Scrum master if they raise an issue that they believe requires attention. No matter where they sit within the organisation, they must be part of the discussion and, therefore, the solution. If the Scrum master doesn't listen, they can't explain how the problem affects them and their team.' I saw realisation cross Leon's face.

'All learnings that arise from this process are essential for informing future decisions in the organisation, so, just like the board itself, these should be accessible to everyone. Keep people informed and updated by email once a month and let them know what improvements have been made and what the key learnings are.'

'You know, for a digital business, we're not as good as we could be at internal comms,' Sabine observed.

'That's because we've not had a structure – no, we've not had a *reason*, to analyse and share this type of information,' Christoph responded. 'We're good at congratulating ourselves when we manage to win a big contract and everyone's straight down to Holl's Bier Kellar that night to celebrate. But we're not that good at telling the rest of the business what's really going on, are we? Come on, be honest.'

'Sadly, I'm inclined to agree,' Herman said. 'What I like about what I'm hearing now is that it's up to *all* of us to be part of the problem solving. I think that greater level of transparency and accountability will make an enormous difference to everyone in the business.'

As we broke for lunch, I looked around the room and sensed that, for some, this need for greater transparency across the entire organisation was a new concept. At the least, it was a broadening out of their current practice. That's one problem organisations with a silo mentality and structure struggle with, because by their nature they funnel their attention toward a narrow focus, not just in terms of inter-company communications but in all aspects of their functionality. This closes off opportunities within those organisations for people with shared interests to come together and resolve issues, improve skills and learn from each other's experiences through CoPs. It was evident to me that this tool was something that was missing within the culture at FSS.

THE ADAPT METHODOLOGY™ PROJECT TO PRODUCT SCORECARD

Eight sessions completed. Evaluate whether you are leading an outdated project-centric business or a modern product-led company at: https://bit.ly/Scorecard_ProductFirst_Book

9

Organisational Mastery – Part Three

We returned to the boardroom, the team having had time to respond to emails and refuel from the sandwich buffet. It was interesting to see how, during the break, they'd mingled more freely, having conversations in pairs and then breaking to speak to somebody else, or call over a colleague to join them. This seemed natural, unforced and more unified; it created a warm energy that was quite different to when I'd first walked through the doors. As they took their seats, I turned to Christoph and said: 'Over lunch, you mentioned to me that there's not a great culture in FSS for communicating things to the people that matter.'

'Yes, I believe that to be true,' he confirmed.

'I guess, then, that there's also not much of a learning culture?'

'That depends on what you mean,' he said.

'No Communities of Practice?'

'Not that I know of. Would I know about them?' he asked.

'Absolutely. They can generate new products and spread best practices among employees. Any organisation with CoPs can expect to rapidly and effectively increase its success compared to their competitors.'

'That's a big claim,' Freddie said.

'No, not a claim – the impact of CoPs is widely measurable.'

'Name me one example,' Freddie challenged me. I smiled and said, 'OK, how about I name five?'

'You have an answer to everything,' Freddie laughed, sitting back in his chair and folding his arms. I ran through the following points.

OM Component 4: Communities of Practice (CoP)

1. Eases newly hired employees into the business. CoP serves as a mentor in helping them understand their role and the importance of their work in the company, increasing their sense of belonging.

2. Projects with CoP backing are executed faster because of employee buy-in – they feel as if they

have personal involvement. It feels different to simply following top–down orders.

3. Members of CoPs think outside of the box in creating additional services and products.

4. CoPs help recruit and retain talent and easily identify which employees are competent and can work productively with others.

5. CoPs are the first line of defence and can turn weaknesses into strengths.

'Is this compulsory?' Jonas asked. Sabine seemed surprised at the question.

'I'd say it's essential, not compulsory,' I replied. 'It depends on what sort of culture FSS wants to foster. Personally, I favour the voluntary approach because that means people *want* to be part of it and also because they know it's supported by the executive team. It tells them that you're open and willing to invest in their knowledge capital.'

'We should be implementing it as a matter of course. We've still got people here who joined us at the beginning; they know everything there is to know about this company, probably more than me,' Herman said. 'What's the first step?'

'Ideally, they should be established through regular collaboration, but in the early stages, initiating and encouraging your people to make CoPs can be a bit challenging. They first have to want to share their thoughts, but if they're not used to doing that within the current culture, they might be reticent.'

'That would be frustrating,' Herman said.

'You can address this head on. I have a ten-point plan to help introduce CoPs into your organisation,' I said, calling up the next set of slides, which outlined the following points:

1. Establish a clear plan or 'structure' – this shows everyone how the CoP will function and what the expectations are. Create a charter or rules of engagement where you identify the group's strategy, communication techniques and scheduling of meetings. Remember: this structure should not alienate the informal, social nature of CoPs – don't suffocate people with rules.

2. Arrange an introductory meeting – members should be able to meet one another on or offline and discuss their goals and objectives. This also gives them the chance to gain more confidence in sharing their ideas and knowledge with the others, which helps enhance the effectiveness of the CoP in the long run. It's a social learning community.

3. Hold meetings on a regular basis – make sure that you give the CoP the time to meet during working hours and publish the schedule to maintain momentum.

4. Project management software tools, such as Basecamp, Asana, Trello and Workplace, can become the community's virtual headquarters.

Members can share documents, delegate tasks, keep track of deadlines and be kept updated with a community calendar. Most importantly, they can extend and continue the conversation, meaning the community is well organised and can stay on-task even if some members participate remotely.

5. Survey your employees to define actual problems – this allows the organisation to learn about its most pressing issues or weaknesses, which CoP members can then focus on, allocating time and resources to tackle them during their regular meetings. It's an indirect way to spark a conversation, maintaining the social learning nature of CoPs.

6. Identify a clear objective / purpose – members will have a good understanding of what they need to do and how to achieve the desired results.

7. Remain aware of the core knowledge and experience that each member brings to the table and can share with the others. The community should comprise a diverse group of people with individual expertise. This can be particularly useful if you're building a company-wide learning community and where at least one member can represent each department. Also identify those who excel in certain areas or have particular skill sets.

8. Appoint a knowledgeable and widely appreciated moderator – they will be vital to the success of the community. Their tasks should include providing guidance during meetings and liaising between the community and the organisation. This appointment can either be made directly or by holding a group vote.

9. Use online forums and social media to stay in touch – online platforms are a convenient and fast way for members to arrive at new and innovative solutions. These should be opt-in only so that it's not seen as an invasion of their social media use.

10. Offer resources and support to help CoPs thrive. This can include tools, apps and sometimes funding. This support is particularly useful in the beginning stages, as CoPs need to develop training and strategies to create solutions that will benefit the company as a whole.

'So these CoPs are completely independent and ideally voluntary?' Freddie asked.

'Yes, but they should be embedded within your organisational structure to ensure that they meet their objectives and can be truly helpful in furthering the company's agenda,' I replied. 'If membership is voluntary, cooperation is much higher.'

'Is there an ideal size?' Leon asked.

'There's no limit in terms of the number of people who can participate,' I said. 'The more the better, because the potential for the company's growth lies within the people working for it. Nurture them and show that, as executive leaders, you're willing to listen to and discuss their suggestions. This can often lead to drastic but positive changes in the company. A CoP normally has a much longer life than a project team or task force. It continues because they share a common interest in a particular domain. They're all committed to their designated area in which to collaborate with other employees to help bring about improvement and develop strategies to overcome relevant hurdles within the company.'

'You mean for years we've hired external consultants to problem-solve when we had all the required expertise right under our noses?' Freddie said, looking faintly sickened.

'Most probably, yes,' I said, confirming his fear.

'Think of all the money we've wasted,' he said, looking glum.

'In many ways,' I added, 'members of a CoP will be more aware of the impacts of your product on consumers. Often, they're the best people to resolve customers' issues.' Freddie shook his head in dismay.

I continued: 'CoPs enable knowledge-sharing within a specific area across the entire organisation. They can also help come up with new product ideas from a fresh perspective, drawing on their knowledge and expertise, targeting new audiences while still pursuing the company's objectives. They're not limited to solving problems, provided you keep supporting, listening to and nurturing them. Without your continued buy-in, they won't last and you'll lose access to one of your best assets – your people.'

'It's like tapping into a free-flow information network we didn't know we had access to, one that can come up with creative solutions,' Herman observed.

'The trick,' I added, 'is to keep things simple and informal, since all members of the CoP have professional obligations. Allow their creativity and ideas to flow naturally and in their own time; don't overburden them with meetings or they'll be exhausted and unproductive. When they feel appreciated, they'll feel motivated.'

'That's all very well and I understand the theory behind it, but does it really work?' Freddie asked. One or two of the others looked a little shocked.

'You're right to ask,' I told him, 'and the answer is yes. The value contributed by CoPs is easily measured.'

'Listening hasn't been one of our strengths, lately,' Herman observed, 'and what we need now are fresh ideas to take this business forward. I'll personally make facilitating CoPs my number one priority. There are people working for us I don't know anything about; I want to change that.'

'I'll support you,' Sabine said, followed by Leon and Jonas.

'I've got some great talent in my team,' Leon said, 'and I'd like to keep as many of them as possible. I've lost at least six in the last two years, really bright and hard-working people.'

'Why did they go?' Herman, asked, puzzled. 'Was it money?'

'Not in all cases. In their exit interviews, a couple of them mentioned that they felt under-utilised and wanted bigger challenges. I had nothing I could offer them.'

'That's disappointing to hear,' Herman said. 'Do you know where they went?'

'One ended up retraining altogether, and Peter went to Deutsche Data. He's a team leader now,' Leon told him.

'What could we have done to keep him?' Herman asked.

'Valued him more, I suppose,' Leon replied.

'Your people feeling valued is the central ethos behind CoPs,' I explained, 'because it motivates them. It also feeds innovation from within that's perfectly aligned to the company strategy.'

We broke for ten minutes. Of all the sessions we'd done so far, this one on CoPs seemed to have had the most sobering effect on the people in the room, Herman especially. As they chatted, I could hear them all telling similar stories to Leon's. This lack of employee engagement and involvement was, evidently, a bigger problem than anybody had realised. If left unchecked, FSS would find itself facing even greater difficulties internally as their talent drained away.

As they settled back in the room, I made an observation: 'It's always concerning when a team loses a highly skilled individual to another job. It's not always down to the money; often, it's because that person feels like their potential to shine hasn't been maximised. Having innovation as a key part of your strategic growth plans is an excellent way to bridge that divide. It's good for the employees – it keeps them aligned, motivated and engaged – and, ultimately, it's good for the business because it can deliver new product to the market, faster, generating revenue. The shift away from project to product allows innovation to be a central part of your transformation, both in terms of structure and future success.'

'It's such a long process though,' Jonas observed, 'how do we keep the momentum going?'

'What if the human side of the operation is the bottleneck? What if I told you that, if you address that, innovations can happen in just one week?' I suggested.

'I think none of us would believe you. We all know the pressures we're under to innovate, and it takes time,' Freddie said.

'And money,' Leon added.

'Of course, and responding to an ever-changing market creates its own pressure. Those types of demands can be tough on any business. But there is a solution,' I insisted.

'If you're about to teach us about Google Design Sprints and design thinking, we've been there,' Freddie interrupted – helpfully, as it happened.

OM Component 5: Design sprints

'And…?' I waited for his reply.

'They have been proven to increase some operational efficiency – not all the time, but we have seen some encouraging results. Though we each measure these in our own areas, not on a cross-functional basis. I'm guessing you're about to tell us we're doing it all wrong?' he smiled at me, ruefully.

'Maybe. My instinct is that when you make it part of your organisational mastery framework, Google Design Sprints meet the challenges in a more holistic fashion. Every team can manage these challenges to create a systematic method toward innovative, tried and tested solutions, since the framework focuses on the users, the business and technology. It's a thinking session to overcome major business and product roadblocks that involves prototyping and testing new ideas or even designs.'

'Some of those roadblocks are huge,' Leon observed.

'The scale of the problem is irrelevant,' I replied. 'The focus of this method is how blockers should be addressed and overcome, given the time and resource constraints.'

'You're talking about a matter of days, though,' Freddie said. 'How can that be?'

'I'll explain Google's five-day method. It's a straightforward, result-oriented process,' I replied.

'Five days? Are you sure?' Freddie pressed me further.

'Yes, achieved in five stages, spearheaded by the sprint master, who defines the problem and works to resolve the challenge. Here's how.' I turned to my laptop and called up the first slide and explained the following stages.

1. Understand

The first part of the sprint is to clearly understand what the problem is and how to solve it. This phase involves rapid ideas-sharing lasting no longer than fifteen minutes, with the ideas collected by the sprint master.

Team members generate ideas using the 'how might we' (HMW) method. They write their thoughts on paper. For example, 'HMW help our users find the relevant page that they're looking for?' or 'HMW make our navigation clear and intuitive for the users?' The phrase 'how might we' is useful because it helps put team members in the right mindset, allowing them to find creative ideas and answers to achieve solutions to the problem.

2. Sketch

The creators of Google Sprint, Jake Knapp, Braden Kowitz, and John Zeratsky,[17] found that sketching is the best way to turn abstract ideas into a plan of action. This enables the team to explore and design different ways of tackling the user's problem. Creative ideas are often produced in concentrated mindset, so team members are given the time to write solutions on their own, everyone then shares their ideas with the group and these are then voted on. Any sketches

---

[17] B Kowitz, J Knapp and J Zeratsky, *Sprint: How to solve big problems and test new ideas in just five days* (Simon & Schuster, 2016)

that are not feasible or will not help solve the user problem are eliminated.

3. Decide

From the ideas that remain, the team discuss and decide which are the best solutions to the problem and these are again put to a vote. Where there is no clear agreement, the group will work toward finding consensus using a decision matrix approach to narrow down the options. The matrix is a simple diagram that helps judge the contender ideas based on a set of requirements that are deemed to be the most useful in meeting the objectives of the whole sprint. The team will then weigh up the risk versus the reward/value of each idea/solution.

4. Prototype

The team is separated into small groups and assigned to different tasks. There are creators, writers, designers and a tester to run the user testing and collate and report on the feedback. The first step is to build a basic functional prototype that tests the ideas on actual users so you can then collect their feedback. View the prototype as a challenging experiment to test out your hypothesis, so think critically about what to build first.

211

5. Validate

Launch the prototype to real users outside the team and gather feedback on what does / doesn't work. The team will conduct interviews and observe users as they try out the prototype, identifying any major issues with the design as revealed through user behaviour. User feedback will be collected throughout, enabling the team to learn different ways to design solutions in line with the defined strategy. Once validation is complete, the team reviews and refines the findings in readiness for presentation, when the results are discussed in order to absorb the learnings and agree the next steps.

'That's a much more streamlined approach than perhaps we've been following,' Freddie said, sounding almost impressed.

'Which means it saves time and valuable resources,' I said.

'It's a much more collaborative and democratic approach, too,' Leon observed.

I agreed, 'And so it's important to remember that although a Google sprint might just be trying to solve one problem in the business, that one problem, if left unsolved, can have an impact on everyone, directly or indirectly. Every sprint should have an action list of learnings leading into the next session of product development.'

'I'm in favour of defining strategy, building basic prototypes,' Jonas said, 'and then collecting feedback as quickly as this approach allows.'

'The feedback process is key to the success of the sprint,' I said, 'because it's inextricably linked to the product discovery we talked about.'

'Do they work in tandem?' Christoph asked.

'The design sprint is the culmination of the entire product discovery stage, which takes place over a week.'

'Achieving what?' Leon asked.

'Imagine, throughout discovery your team has been taking feedback from customers as iterations are released into market so by the time the sprint arrives, that's when you can bring your assumptions into an intense period of innovation, validating, or not, those assumptions in real time, with real customers.'

'We'll see in no time at all whether that prototype is a workable solution,' Freddie observed.

'Or not,' Leon clarified.

'It does away with the hierarchy too,' Herman noted. 'I should be as much a part of these sprints as anyone else so that everyone can see that I'm working alongside them to find solutions. The voting mechanism is great. It's never going to be the leader's final decision and nobody should feel pressurised to agree with what I, or any of us, think.'

'I think it shows greater levels of trust and transparency right across the board,' Sabine added.

'Literally,' Herman agreed.

'We should be making it clearer that we value the opinions of our people,' Christoph said. 'This is just right. Anything that contributes to a better team spirit and greater cooperation in the company can only be a good thing.'

'I'd also add,' I said, 'that this process opens up a treasure trove of useful and creative ideas that might never have been discovered otherwise. What this method does is train you as a business to flex your creative muscles and generate new solutions, all the while placing the users' needs as top priority. Before closing the sprint, the sprint master will invite everyone to a closing circle and ask the participants for their takeaways and insights from the experience. It's essential to make participants feel that they've each accomplished a significant mission after the sprint. Everyone's ideas from day one have contributed to the solution and that should be cause for celebration.'

'And to carry those learnings into the business going forward,' Sabine remarked.

'Not only that, but it stops us from wasting time and resources,' Christoph added.

'How do you work that out?' Leon asked.

'Assuming we've gone through the initial process of product discovery, then at the end of the quarterly development cycle that concludes with the design sprint we'll have validation of whether the customer wants the product. They might not, at which point we can decide to discard that particular feature – and that's okay, too.'

'Of course,' Leon said, 'and so, if customers tell us they want it, the next week we can create the OKRs for the upcoming cycle to fully develop the feature, as we have that validation.'

'Which isn't, therefore, part of the product backlog. This is going to create so much more space for us. It's the piece of the Agile puzzle we've been missing,' Christoph concluded.

'Well, I've learned something today,' Freddie said. Everyone turned toward him expectantly and he paused for effect before continuing, 'I always thought Agile was mostly about consultants rocking up with their PowerPoint presentations and regurgitating some irrelevant nonsense that they learned in business school, then buggering off and costing us a fortune in the process. Actually, what they showed us makes quite a bit of sense, except very little of it works in relation to product. Projects, yes. But where has projects got us? A bit of progress here, a few steps back there. We've been standing still working away on our own projects, all in good faith, yet there's been nothing to connect us all together in working toward the same goals. Yes, we meet as a board on a regular basis, and we pat ourselves on the backs because we've managed to keep our heads above water – against all the odds, I might add – and we convince ourselves we have a strategic vision.'

'Don't we?' Herman asked.

'Of course we do. We all know where we want FSS to be in the future, but what do I know about how Leon tries to achieve the vision? Or Christoph? Any of us. What do you know about how I work ten hours a day trying to keep IT on track? We're all doing great things by ourselves for our departments, and we think that, by doing that, we're doing great things for the business. We're not, though, are we? We spend most of our time pulling in different directions.'

'To be fair,' I interrupted, 'FSS isn't alone in that. Many businesses still operate along those traditional lines.'

'In silos, yes,' Freddie said. 'And that's what I've learned – that we all knew we needed to change, we just didn't know how. If we implement any or all of what Luis has described, it won't be easy, but to quote what he said earlier, we need to measure not just the risk versus the reward, but the *value* we'll create for the business if we do make these changes.'

'I agree,' Herman said. 'The risk to this business of rejecting the idea of OM is that in two years' time, we won't be meeting at all.'

Herman's words hung in the air as the others took in the gravity of the situation.

'It is a big moment,' I said, 'and it takes the introduction to organisational mastery at this stage in the workshop to realise how that transformation can be achieved. You have the framework and the glue to put it all together now, knowing what fits where and why. The next and final session, on data, will be the icing on the cake.'

THE ADAPT METHODOLOGY™
PROJECT TO PRODUCT SCORECARD

Nine sessions completed. Evaluate whether you are leading an outdated project-centric business or a modern product-led company at: https://bit.ly/Scorecard_ProductFirst_Book

10

Data

The last session I run on the final day is short, but impactful. Over the three days of the workshop I've been privileged to have held the attention of a dynamic, if somewhat dysfunctional, executive leadership team. One that agreed to take time out from their schedules and responsibilities to listen and engage with me as I presented a series of mindset-shifting challenges and home truths. By now I've introduced them to the majority of my ADAPT Methodology™ turning their expectations of Agile upside down in the process, so that they can begin to build an operational and infrastructure strategy that will take their business forward in the digital age. They've been reassured that there's no need to reinvent the entire company, but I have prompted them to think differently about what their core business is, their product. This is their transformation. How they evaluate the data that springs from that transformation will be key to their ongoing success, as data offers the best insights into both business performance and customer behaviour. The reason why I leave this until the final session will soon become clear to them.

The data pillar is an amalgamation of the other ADAPT Methodology™ pillars. It was essential to gain their buy-in to the other four pillars before we reached this point, as this would be key to their understanding of the five layers of data I was about to outline.

'Will there be any surprises here?' Freddie asked.

'Yes,' I replied simply. This was my cue to introduce the first layer and I pulled up a slide with the first heading: 'Engagement metrics'.

'This is the beginning of your data journey,' I explained, 'where you will discover the areas where potential customers stop engaging with your product. These metrics will surprise you, especially if you've never fully engaged with the concept of continuous discovery,' I told them. 'For example, you should track customer behaviour and question why they go no further down the sales pipeline even though they've visited your site, wandered through your social media, downloaded a whitepaper or read one of your blogs.'

'Easy – because they're boring,' Freddie snapped, 'even I can't be bothered to read them.' Christoph looked mildly shocked, perhaps offended – the content was currently his responsibility. Maybe Freddie was speaking the truth.

'That's for you to discover, but they may have subscribed to your feed or even trialled a product sample, yet still failed to convert to meaningful sales. What does that tell you?'

'That maybe Freddie's right. Either our content is shit or our product offering is,' Christoph said.

'Or both?' Jonas added. Judging by the smirks and laughter, he might have hit the nail on the head. One thing is for sure: had I introduced the data pillar on Day One, I don't think they would have been as frank in their responses.

'We'll come onto that,' I said, before calling up the next slide and heading: 'Product usage'.

'Assuming that not all potential customers share Jonas' opinion – because some do convert into paid customers at various levels, be that basic, premium or enterprise products – these metrics offer insights into how they then use those products, and for how long. That information is vital to improve retention going forward.'

'We've seen quite a bit of churn, even from day one,' Christoph noted.

'What's your response to that?' I asked him.

'Send them discounts, special bundles, upgrades, that kind of thing.'

'What's the take-up like?' I pressed him further.

'Some do, some don't,' he said, sounding a little defeated.

'Do you know what contributes to the churn?'

'Not really,' Christoph admitted. 'We've always believed that our product range is good – really good, in fact – but our competitors undercut us. It's probably a price thing.'

'In which case, you've mainly been reactive, not basing your response on any actual data analysis?' I suggested.

'I guess that's true,' he concurred.

'You could be more proactive, then?' To which he nodded his agreement. 'Which perhaps says more about your content than your product,' I mused. The room looked thoughtful. I break the silence.

'Data tells you when customers fall away. Data also tells you where you need to improve engagement.'

'We do that anyway, but the gains are only ever marginal,' Sabine protested.

'Then we obviously need to do better,' Herman said curtly. Sabine looked surprised by his tone.

'To be fair,' I replied, 'you've not had the benefit of a context where data fits into the entire strategy. This is why I leave data to the last session – all too often, business leaders will rush headlong to the data in the expectation that it will provide all the answers, without first asking the right questions.'

'Such as, "do we need to be publishing better content based on customers' needs, or putting more information out there?"' Christoph said.

'Yes, but I've also seen businesses bombarding customers with too much content. Data analysis will unlock those questions,' I reassured him, moving on to the next slide: 'Completed actions'.

I then asked the group to think about the total number of actions the customer performs as part of their engagement with FSS. 'The outcome should be an understanding of which features are being used and which are not,' I explained.

'I can tell you that straightaway,' Freddie said. 'One example is that a significant number of customers who use our invoicing software only make use of that one application.'

'What are they not using that they could be?' I asked.

'We've built a great feature that offers reimbursements as an automated process but there's only been a small take-up, proportionally. It's part of our enterprise package, whereas our premium reminder feature is used quite widely.'

'You have that data already? What have you done with it?'

'Offered it out as a bundle, but even then, the take-up is low by comparison.'

'Perhaps it's not a feature the market wants, in that case? Was it tested in the discovery cycle, like we covered?'

'No,' Freddie said, 'we just assumed it would appeal.'

'I don't think we'll be making that assumption again,' Herman said.

'It might not be a mistake, just not right for your current customer base,' I countered, 'but if you put it through the product discovery cycle while testing it with your expanded clientele, you may find the resulting data about what the customer needs and wants tells you a different story,' I suggested.

Freddie mumbled in what seemed to be agreement and jotted down some thoughts on his notepad.

'Isn't this the same point as in the previous slide?' Sabine asked, when I pulled up the next heading: 'Usage behaviour'.

'Not quite; there's a nuanced difference,' I explained. 'It's more related to how the user is actually using the software, in respect of flow.'

'You mean, what catches their attention, prompting them to click through?'

'Exactly,' I said.

'Literally tracking their mouse movements, in that case,' Sabine added.

'Not quite as Orwellian as that, but it does involve tracking behaviour and how the users interact with the software so that you can detect patterns.'

'I'm not sure I understand what that means, or how you do it,' Herman said.

'It's like stepping into their shoes and following their journey. For example, do they click more frequently on the left-hand side of the screen, or on the right?' I explained.

'Once we understand that, we can place features or software upgrades in the space they gravitate to, I presume?' Leon said, thinking aloud, 'Which would then lead to greater take-up?'

I nodded. 'It's similar to how supermarkets set out their aisles, which is a science in itself, based on huge amounts of customer psychology research that helps them to identify where best to place special offers, or how to position items to prompt an impulse purchase.

The same principle can be applied to how users navigate websites.'

'Maybe our "recently added" features are in the wrong part of our site?' Sabine wondered. 'But analysing the data will tell us literally where to point customers to, to increase engagement and generate more conversions.'

'And then measure the results,' I added.

The last slide – 'Product insights' – showed how a team of data science engineers would extrapolate the data from the previous four layers to analyse and interpret the resultant insights using data science technology.

'Isn't this what the first four layers do?' Freddie asked, with a quizzical look.

'This takes data analysis to another level, with an eye to the future. The insights they gain from user behaviours throughout the previous layers will generate a whole new range of potential features and products designed to appeal to the customer.'

'How?' Christoph asked.

'Data engineers have the skills to tell you in specific detail the things that retain a user's attention or prompt them to click. Not only that, but they also measure that behaviour over a period of time so that patterns of flow become visible, such as where drop-off occurs. They can identify the types of customers you retain for just two months, as opposed to three years. That information is in the data you've already generated, but because it sits within individual departmental silos that don't cross-communicate, it's never analysed from the right perspective. In truth, the data you collect right now is worth very little within your current operation, when it could be a highly valuable resource if you connect all the dots.'

'We can identify that already by picking over data layers one to four?' Herman asked. 'That would tell us where to add new features, or upsell?'

I nodded. 'It's so obvious,' he said, 'all this time we've been sat on a pot of gold without knowing it.' He flopped back in his chair, gobsmacked.

'I said there'd be some surprises,' I reminded him, 'generating new business opportunities is just one of them.'

'I thought we were on top of data,' Sabine said, looking at Freddie, who just shrugged in response. She seemed a little peeved, IT being his area of responsibility, but like all of them in the room, Freddie, despite his expertise, had clearly not imagined that data could be so thoroughly interrogated.

'This could have a massive impact on future revenue,' Sabine continued, softening a little. 'Look, I'm not blaming anyone. We've all had our brains fried with new insights these last few days. I'm just disappointed that we haven't performed to our optimal capability. This is a collective responsibility, after all – Freddie, I'm not having a go at you.'

'What's the biggest mistake the business has been making?' I asked her.

'Thinking we're a digital business because we sell digital solutions. Clearly, we're not. We've been operating more like a shoe shop.'

Despite the critique, the room broke into laughter.

'I think that's harsh, but fair,' Herman concluded when the room quietened down again. 'We've taken our eye off the ball. Luis, what do you suggest?'

'For starters, creating a dashboard that's visible to the entire company that clearly shows data layers one to three,' I said.

'Why not all five?' Freddie asked.

'Because they're more about generating insights that inform business ideas and new features. Having a dashboard showing the first three layers for every product will enable the business to be more proactive in real time. Reactive solutions are usually too little, too late to create any real impact.'

'What upsets me,' Christoph interjected, 'is that four years ago we launched a totally new product and it did pretty well, generating several million in revenue. We looked at the sales and marketing data – those first two layers you've shown us today – and the numbers were great. We were all pleased with ourselves, but then it tailed off and now it's just one of our average performers. We couldn't understand what it was that left it sitting in the doldrums. Yes, we made a decent ROI, but it wasn't the bright star we all hoped it would be. Now I'm thinking, what more could we have achieved if we'd added in data layers three to five? Maybe we'd have gone from 3 million to 5 million in those four years because we understood what the data was telling us about customer behaviour. Even if we recruited a few expensive data scientists, it would have been worthwhile because the ROI we'd have achieved would have been so much better.' He sat back in his seat, folded his arms and stared at his notepad.

'It proves that you not only need data science, but you can trust it,' I said. 'Transforming the revenue stream to an upward curve takes investment in experts who can do the analysis so that you can benefit.'

Through the three-day workshop with FSS, my aim was to show that the operational and strategic shift from projects to products is a game changer for businesses of any shape or size looking to thrive in the digital era. Whereas the traditional silo approach works toward an outcome that often falls short of expectations, the lean approach in my ADAPT Methodology™ is a continuous and evolving process that maximises discovery and innovation. With a complete data strategy built-in from day one of the process, as opposed to a back-end data analysis approach, the business gains a real-time view of the relationship between its products and its customers. This allows the business to stay ahead of the curve instead of falling behind it. This was the single biggest issue facing FSS and its plans to grow and scale and why it was stagnating in the face of its more agile competition.

THE ADAPT METHODOLOGY™
PROJECT TO PRODUCT SCORECARD

Ten sessions completed. Evaluate whether you are leading an outdated project-centric business or a modern product-led company at: https://bit.ly/Scorecard_ProductFirst_Book

The outcome

Once my final session and the three-day workshop had come to a thought-provoking conclusion, Herman joined me in private.

'I didn't know what to expect,' he said, 'but I believe we've got a greater degree of clarity on the tasks ahead. Not just about what we urgently need to do to get us fit for the digital market, but we also know much more about who we are and what our product is.' I was pleased with his progress and gratified by his endorsement.

'For me, the reward was also in seeing how your colleagues underwent their own transformations.'

'You mean Freddie?' Herman laughed. 'He can be a little difficult. He's a bigger Agile fan than any of us now.'

'Barriers to change are never usually the people themselves,' I said, 'they've been indoctrinated by the culture created by silo-led organisations. They feel the need to protect, or defend, their role, but what organisational mastery teaches us is that when departments coalesce to work as one team dedicated to product, the project mentality pales by comparison.'

'I see that now,' Herman said. 'I also see where we've strayed from our strategic vision by focusing too much on projects. It's created so many backlogs and conflicts, we all lost sight of the desired outcomes.'

'This is the perfect opportunity for the business to better understand its customers' behaviour. If and when you decide to implement the ADAPT Methodology™, my expectation is that the business will be fit for the digital future and will achieve great success. It's a transformative process.'

As I left the building to head for the taxi waiting to take me back to Munich, Herman and I continued to walk and talk. 'Luis, when I first reached out to you, I knew that we had issues to overcome within the business if we ever hoped to scale and grow. At the time, I didn't realise that a number of those issues lay within the leadership team.'

'That wasn't because you had a weak team,' I reassured him, 'it was because the business itself was stuck operating in much more of an analogue way while trying to push a digital product. In the digital era, that's not possible. You've built an incredibly successful business from scratch, but since it was founded fifteen years ago, things have changed.'

'Yes, technology for one,' he agreed.

'More than that. Customers have changed too, be they consumer or corporate. Their purchasing habits have radically altered and so have their expectations.'

'Yes, I was intrigued when you began the workshop with the Approach pillar. That made us all think, Freddie especially. I'm relieved he came around in the end.'

'I understood exactly where he was coming from, though,' I said.

'You did?' Herman smiled.

'Agile is one of those "love it or hate it" processes that people either adopt straightaway, or they run a mile from because they don't see the point. It depends entirely on why a business needs to be more Agile but, more importantly, how it's then implemented. You've seen for yourself that Agile hasn't yet worked for FSS.'

'I never understood why that was,' he replied.

'If it's just another exercise, then it has no meaning and no impact. Especially if it's not embedded at the heart of the company's strategic vision. Agile is there to accelerate that, not impede it by creating more projects and teams that bear little or no relevance to product.'

'Your workshop on product and the need to continually discover, deliver and deploy was a bit of a gamechanger for us all. We're so used to working in project teams here, developing products over a lengthy period without the incremental gains that you've shown us can make all the difference to our customers and our revenue.'

'That's when Freddie began to come around,' I reflected. 'I think he's probably a fantastic project leader, one who really homes in on the detail and knows where he wants to be heading. He has an outcome in mind but, because of ingrained practices here – the silo mentality – he was the king of the castle. He was determined to see a project through, but his blind spots prevented him from seeing the bigger picture. That's the difference with ADAPT – the sole focus is product.'

'And not project,' Herman said.

My taxi arrived.

Herman opened the door for me but, before I climbed in, he looked at me directly and asked, 'Would you be willing to lead us through our transformation?'

I was delighted that Herman had extended this invitation because it demonstrated that he was ready and willing to fully commit. 'Of course,' I replied. 'We have a full team ready to step in and engage with you.'

'I'm relieved to hear you say that. We've failed for so many years; we don't want to fail again. We've all worked too hard to fall behind.'

'I don't pretend it will be easy, especially when it comes to your organisational mastery. Remember, you'll be implementing this new process in parallel with the current business operations, so it will be an evolving picture for a while.'

'I understand. But we want to grow, not contract. You've shown us the *why*, now we need the *how*. To be honest, we wouldn't have a clue how to make it all happen. We understand what needs to be achieved, but we need help getting there.'

'In that case, I'd be happy to,' I said, smiling. Herman stretched out his arm to shake my hand and with that, we said our goodbyes.

Conclusion

If you had wondered at the beginning why I chose to write this book in this form, I hope you now see it was the right decision. So much of what I do is about helping a business develop its own story in respect of how it operates, because behind every product, there are people. My work isn't simply about presenting a process, because often the blockages arise when I butt up against certain rigidly traditional mindsets. I don't judge people for that, I only ever try to help them think differently, specifically away from projects and toward product. The ADAPT Methodology™ only comes into play once that mindset has shifted. By communicating its principles in story form, I have been able to share the typical journeys of the many teams I have encountered in all types of digitally led businesses, in a more impactful way. There is always a Freddie, but there's always a Herman too, someone who is desperate to turn things around but doesn't have the answers. In a leadership team where there is friction and entrenched practices, conflict and confusion can arise and the outcomes, for either the individuals or the business, tend not to be positive.

Herman and his team had been too focused on delivering output through an endless cycle of projects that consistently failed to deliver strong returns. Project-oriented organisations are primarily concerned with delivering results on time and on budget, but that doesn't guarantee the results they're hoping for. Becoming a 'product first' organisation is the game changer that opens the gateway to a sustainable and continuously revenue-generating future for a business that understands the correlation between outcome and impact.

Helping businesses like the fictional FSS to achieve organisational mastery is one of my greatest rewards. For 'Herman' and his colleagues, their biggest learning outcomes were that, in 'product first' organisations:

- The product (value streams) is at the core, not projects

- The focus is on outcome, not output

- Budgets are assigned to OKRs and products, not to departments

- A lean approach enables OKRs to feed the product backlog

- Continuous product discovery is key to ongoing development and review of the business strategy

- Inter-departmental dependencies are broken through building value streams that contain the full skill set required to deliver a product

Projects versus products

Projects – traditional budgeting	Products – lean budgeting
• Defined by its output	• Defined by how it is used by end users
• Doesn't always have standalone value	• Always has standalone value to end users
• Temporary	• Long lived (until it no longer meets an end-user need)
• Ramp-up teams, ramp down teams	• Long-lived teams
• Output focused	• Impact and outcomes focused
• Fixed requirements	• Evolving needs
• 'Change control' process	• Rapidly pivot and adapt to changing needs
• Led by a project manager	• Led by a product manager
• Value delivered at the end	• Value delivered iteratively
• Handed over to a business owner	• Continuous deliver of value to end users
• Learnings at the end	• Continuous learning and improvement
• Report on activity and output – deliverables, time, budget	• Report on value – impact and outcomes

There are many digital organisations that, like FSS, believe they are digital yet are mystified when the digital marketplace fails to live up to their expectations. It's only because of my years of experience working within this landscape and the ability to take several steps back to analyse how it has developed and changed (usually at a rapid pace), that I've been able to create the ADAPT Methodology™ and put it into practice. I've seen it transform the practice and ROI of many organisations, from across Europe to the Middle East. It would be easy to believe that the digital era presents a global opportunity to trade in every corner of the world, but it's an error to assume that 'global' means 'one size fits all'. For a business to expand and scale into territories beyond its home, knowing how to approach, attract and convert that global marketplace into customers relies on the business adopting a 'product first' mentality and identifying the fundamental principles in each territory before it can truly have a global impact.

If that's your ambition for your organisation, I can help you achieve this. I invite you to get in touch at www.adaptmethodology.com and share with me your vision so we can begin a conversation. Or if, like Herman, you are interested to learn more about the workshop described in this book, you can download the brochure at: bit.ly/ADAPT_Workshop_Product-First_Book

To be continued…

Acknowledgements

This book is the result of almost two decades of experience and the guidance of a special friend who pushes me to become better on a daily basis. He has helped me to develop a philosophy to help leaders that is captured by the phrase: 'The simplicity of the actions leads to the simplicity of the results.' I therefore start my acknowledgements with a special mention for Raphael B.

Another great mentor, coach and, above all, great friend is Ezequiel Vasconcellos. I want to thank him for all the support he has provided during the last year of my life. Thanks also to my parents, who were always there supporting me in the most challenging times.

Life achievements are nothing if we cannot share them with our friends, so I dedicate this book to some of my closest friends, all of whom are part of my journey: André Moreiras, Itanara Lima, Mário Figueira, Alvaro Ferreira, Fernanda Vasconcelos, Susana Tomás, Kacau Dias, Ana Santos and Nuno Morgadinho.

A special thanks to my ex-wife Veronika Gonçalves. I would not be where I am today without her help and understanding. She supported me in really difficult times like no one else ever has.

I wouldn't have been able to write this book without the help of the Rethink team and the experience gained while working with my special customers – people like Timo Salzsieder, Vishal Patel, Mishari A Al-Assailan, Ahmed Alenazi, José Pedro Pinto and Ricardo Parreira.

Finally, special thanks to the people that read and provided a praise quote to be included in this book: José Pedro Pinto, Rui Pedro Saraiva, Jorge Afonso, Joao Colaço, Mishari A Al-Assailan and Marcus Nordquist.

The Author

Luis Gonçalves is an entrepreneur, bestselling author and international keynote speaker. He works with entrepreneurs, founders and senior leaders to implement his game-changing ADAPT Methodology®, enabling them to transform traditional project-centric companies into modern digital-product-led businesses. He has been breaking new ground in the software industry for the last two decades, building his business and developing his practice in Europe and beyond. His blog is considered a 'must-read' for anyone in the software development industry.

🌐 https://luis-goncalves.com

🔲 www.facebook.com/lmsgoncalves

🔲 www.linkedin.com/in/luismsg

🔲 www.twitter.com/lgoncalves1979

🔲 @lgoncalves1979 Also by this author

Also by this Author

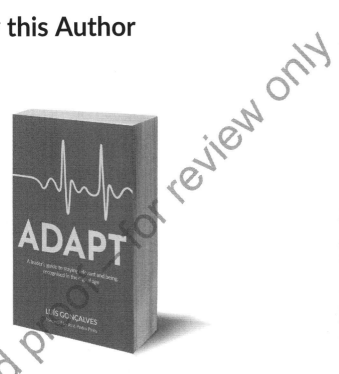